WOMEN AND CHURCH

FAITH & ORDER/USA

FAITH AND ORDER SERIES

Women and Church

*The Challenge of Ecumenical Solidarity
in an Age of Alienation*

Edited by Melanie A. May

Foreword by Monika K. Hellwig

William B. Eerdmans Publishing Co. ♦ Grand Rapids
Friendship Press ♦ New York

For Commission on Faith and Order
National Council of the Churches of Christ in the USA

Copyright © 1991 by Commission on Faith and Order, NCCCUSA
475 Riverside Drive, Room 872, New York, N.Y. 10115-0050
(212) 870-2569

First published 1991 for the Commission on Faith and Order by
Wm. B. Eerdmans Publishing Co.
255 Jefferson Ave. S.E., Grand Rapids, Mich. 49503
and
Friendship Press
475 Riverside Drive, Room 772, New York, N.Y. 10115

Library of Congress Cataloging-in-Publication Data

Women and church: the challenge of ecumenical solidarity in an
    age of alienation / edited by Melanie A. May.
        p.   cm.
    Includes bibliographical references.
    ISBN 0-8028-0552-3 (Eerdmans)
    1. Women and Christian union.   I. May, Melanie A.
BX9.5.W65   1991
270.8′25′082 — dc20   90-27073
                                                              CIP

Friendship Press ISBN 0-337-00235-6

Contents

v

Dedicated

to

Jane Cary Chapman Peck

Associate Professor of Religion and Society at
Andover Newton Theological Seminary

and

Vice President of the
National Council of Churches of Christ in the USA
from 1987 until her death in 1990

Dr. Peck would be pleased to be associated with this book. She was reared in a Methodist home in Georgia, and from early childhood onward was an ecumenist; she was taught to challenge every injustice of racism and classism that surrounded her. Later she came to understand sexism and heterosexism as related evils.

Dr. Peck was a "witness for peace," particularly in Central America, where successive sabbaticals and study projects took her to Costa Rica, Cuba, Nicaragua, and, as a founding member of the Life and Peace Institute, to Uppsala, Sweden. An "internationalist," she was a delegate to the WCC's Assembly in Vancouver and to its conference in Seoul entitled "Justice, Peace and the Integrity of Creation." She held many positions in the NCCC during her twelve years on its governing board, and through it she found many opportunities to link her academic work with justice-seeking in the church and in the world.

Jane Cary's spirit permeates this book, since she deliberately chose her role as lay woman, supported issues that frequently put her at odds with faculty colleagues, challenged every narrow view of the church's life and teaching, and concretely expressed her commitments in the shaping of her home and family. Her name will be added to the list of leaders and martyrs who, when the roll is called, will shout "Presente!" And we will respond to one another—in her spirit, which this book engenders—"Adelante!"

Jeanne Audrey Powers

Jeanne Audrey Powers is Associate General Secretary of the General Commission on Christian Unity and Interreligious Concerns of the United Methodist Church. She was a colleague of Dr. Peck in many ecumenical circles.

Foreword

Monika K. Hellwig

THIS is a volume full of the voices of women. They are voices
that need to be heard, voices that have much to say, that
have long been drowned out, that speak of hope and solidarity,
of peace and common endeavors. Because women in most
churches have for the most part been excluded from ordained
ministry, they have not usually been able to play any official
role in the shaping of the institutional churches or in the ecumenical relations of the institutional churches. But this is not
the only kind of work constitutive of individual churches or of
ecumenical relations and cooperation. At the grass roots women
have been very much involved in church activities, and they
have significant experience and reflection to contribute to the
questions that lie before the Christian churches in our times.
Thus a volume like this one is to be welcomed with open arms
and open hearts and minds. There is much here that offers fresh
insights, raises new questions, and looks at old questions from

*Monika K. Hellwig is past president of the Catholic Theological Society
of America. She is Professor of Systematic Theology at Georgetown
University in Washington, D.C.*

a new angle; there is also much that offers new approaches to the solution of problems both old and new in our complex world.

Because women have for the most part been excluded from roles of dominance in the churches, it may well be that they have learned a more characteristically Christian approach to tasks of leadership—patterns of horizontal leadership or true ministry, leadership by the evoking of consensus, community building in the wisdom of the Holy Spirit. There are advantages as well as disadvantages in speaking from a position of exclusion. Such a position liberates the prophetic function by offering those in the position a more detached view. Such a position also provides protection against arguments based on the authority of office that are not also based on the authority of experience and faithful listening to the experience of others. Moreover, one who speaks from a position of exclusion is more likely to speak on behalf of the excluded and is more likely to speak out of compassion. Of course, women are not always paragons of all these virtues, but they are better placed in relation to them and therefore more likely to exemplify them.

The move for genuine solidarity has tended to come from the poor, the powerless, and the excluded. The voices of the women in this collection give vivid expression to such moves for solidarity with and among the churches, and for solidarity beyond the churches with those who suffer discrimination, oppression, homelessness, joblessness, and every other kind of brutalization. The voices in this book are voices of practical compassion and of practical hope. They are voices that need to be heard.

Preface

Mary Ann Lundy and Forrest C. Stith

THE Ecumenical Decade was declared by the World Council of Churches as a response by the religious community to the unfinished agenda of the United Nations Decade for Women (1975-1985). The council urged churches "to eliminate teachings and practices which discriminate against women as a Christian response to the forward-looking strategies adopted by the UN Conference in Nairobi in 1985."[1]

By taking this action, the council built upon a foundation laid in its earlier history. In particular, it built on "The Com-

1. *World Council of Churches Central Committee, Minutes of the Thirty-Eighth Meeting, Geneva, Switzerland, 16-24 Jan. 1987* (Geneva: World Council of Churches, 1982), p. 70.

Mary Ann Lundy, Co-chair of the U.S. Committee of the Ecumenical Decade: Churches in Solidarity with Women, is Director of the Women's Unit of the Presbyterian Church, U.S.A., headquartered in Louisville, Kentucky.

Forrest C. Stith, Co-chair of the U.S. Committee of the Ecumenical Decade: Churches in Solidarity with Women, is Resident Bishop of the New York West Area, the United Methodist Church.

munity of Women and Men in the Church," a study conducted
from 1978 to 1981. This study invited member communions to
initiate local and regional study groups with the goal of understanding and moving toward partnership at all levels of church
life.

But some now ask, "Why another emphasis on women's
participation in church and in society? We're obviously moving,
and things are better than they were for women. Haven't things
improved for women here and around the world?" They have,
but there is still much room for improvement. While gains have
been made within some churches with regard to the ordination
of women as clergy and laity and while some women have
moved into leadership positions, we still have a long way to go
to reach the goal of full participation of women in the churches.
Women still are not represented in decision-making arenas in
proportion to their membership. Churches still express the
Christian faith in words that exclude women. There is still a
double standard for employment practices. Inequity in salary is
still a reality. Myths and stereotypes that assign second-class
status and roles to women are still perpetuated within churches.
Moreover, while there was great hope that the UN Decade
would effect change for women in society, the truth is that
women are not better off. Indeed, in many areas of their lives
and in most countries, women face more difficult conditions
today than they did twenty years ago. For example, women
workers in industry are regularly paid the lowest wages without
benefits and often without protection. Women in rural areas
regularly receive least attention in development plans and are
not consulted about their basic needs. And, as socio-economic
conditions deteriorate, women are the first to lose their jobs.
As men's accompanying frustration grows, the level of sexual
abuse and violence against women grows.

In light of these facts and much, much more, it is clear that
there is work to be done in the United States and around the
world. During the Ecumenical Decade, churches are challenged

to engage in women's struggles. Churches are challenged to create a sharing, healing, empowering ministry. Churches are challenged to denounce hierarchy and the oppression of women within their own structures. Churches are challenged to share leadership in decision-making, to engage women in contributing to theological reflection and spiritual renewal, and to affirm the exercise of women's gifts in church and community. Churches are challenged to free themselves from racism, sexism, and classism and to model new forms of partnership.

This is an awesome agenda for institutions that historically have often been the slowest to change. Churches have often been the structures most closely identified with a culture that has relegated women to second-class status. The ingratitude of this agenda is deepened by the increasingly conservative movement worldwide.

Yet it is also within the churches that women have many times found their voices. Women in the churches have at times been called into partnership and equipped for meaningful vocations. Claiming this heritage creates hope as we now challenge the churches to live out their message of full personhood for women and men alike and to commit themselves anew to the struggle for liberation for all persons.

The Ecumenical Decade is not a decade of women *for* women. It is not a decade for women in the churches to work for women. The Ecumenical Decade is a time for men and women in the churches to work together to bring about changes in ecclesiastical and social structures that are obstacles to women's full personhood and participation.

The Ecumenical Decade will achieve its goals only if the knowledge, experience, and commitment of women and men are developed into new configurations at local levels. We will need to set priorities in light of local needs and local resources, even as we also work together with an acute awareness of the global context. As we tackle our issues of work and worship in our own places and as we struggle together for solutions to common problems, we will be forging solidarity with sisters and brothers across the continents with whom we share common concerns and commitments.

In 1974, Philip Potter, former General Secretary of the World Council of Churches, spoke to a consultation on sexism held in Berlin. His words are as appropriate for the Ecumenical Decade as they were for that meeting:

> Neither men nor women will become truly human unless this disease of sexism is diagnosed and cured. It will be one world of women and men together or no world at all. And we are still a world in [the] state of becoming. Sexism, like racism, is sin. Only in Christ can we become renewed to be authentic human beings, as men and women. But our life in Christ needs to be made real and manifest in our life together in church and society.[2]

2. *Sexism in the 1970s: Discrimination against Women: Report of a World Council of Churches Consultation, West Berlin, 1974* (Geneva: World Council of Churches, 1975).

Introduction

Melanie A. May

WOMEN and church. For centuries, this conjunction has been fraught with ambiguity. Few would dispute the fact that women have actively participated in the church—have filled the pews, provided hospitality, formed children in the faith, cooked church suppers, visited the sick, raised money for mission, quilted for relief projects, gathered in small groups for prayer and Scripture study. But by now few would dispute the fact that women have too often served from subordinate places in church structures and that the church's theology has cast women as created in God's image only in relation to men, only secondarily.

Women are raising questions about our role and image in the church. These questions are not new to recent decades or to this century. Nearly a hundred years ago, Elizabeth Cady Stanton and Matilda Joselyn Gage, who together with Susan B. Anthony wrote the *History of Woman Suffrage*, were among the

---

Melanie A. May, Ecumenical Officer of the Church of the Brethren, is Chair of the NCC's Commission on Faith and Order and a member of the WCC's Commission on Faith and Order. She is the author of Bonds of Unity: Women, Theology and the Worldwide Church.

most articulate spokeswomen connecting the subordinate status of woman in society to her role in the church and her image as drawn from Scripture. Their books—*The Woman's Bible* and *Woman, Church & State*—are women's classics.[1] In their books these two foremothers argued that the church has been not only the site of but also the seedbed for the suppression women have suffered. Elizabeth Cady Stanton's searing insight was overshadowed when suffrage became the increasingly critical issue for women in the latter days of the nineteenth century. Most women did not dare to connect their desire for the right to vote with any in-depth analysis of church and society. Indeed, the cause of suffrage cast out Cady Stanton's connections between women's disenfranchisement and traditional theological lines of thought. Accordingly, Matilda Joselyn Gage's manifesto, in which she spoke about prehistoric matriarchies that she believed were egalitarian, woman-centered communities that worshipped a female deity, was all but erased from the historical record. After her book was published, former sisters in the struggle came to view Gage as a political liability.

Beginning in the late 1960s, books written by women about the church began to be published again. Foremost among these were *The Church and the Second Sex* by Mary Daly, *Women's Liberation and the Church* by Sally Bentley Doely, and *Adam's Fractured Rib: Observations on Women in the Church* by Margaret Sittler Ermarth. Also important was Nelle Morton's essay entitled "Women's Liberation and the Church," published in *Tempo*.[2] These were ground-breaking works. They expressed

1. See Elizabeth Cady Stanton and the Revising Committee, *The Woman's Bible* (New York: European Publishing Company, 1898); and Matilda Joselyn Gage, *Woman, Church & State: The Original Exposé of Male Collaboration against the Female Sex* (1893; rpt. Watertown, Mass.: Persephone Press, 1980).

2. See Mary Daly, *The Church and the Second Sex* (New York: Harper & Row, 1968); *Women's Liberation and the Church*, ed. Sally Bentley Doely (New York: Association Press, 1970); Margaret Sittler Ermarth, *Adam's Fractured Rib: Observations on Women in the Church* (Philadelphia: Fortress Press, 1970);

brokenness, pain, and rage. They made crucial connections between women's status and the very constitution of the church and its companion theology.

Following the furrows of these ground-breaking books, some women have moved out of the church, many mourning shattered symbols of faith. Others have been motivated to move within the church, seeking reform, reconfiguration, renewal. These decisions—to move out or to motivate for change—have not been made lightly. For many who moved out, the decision was a matter of spiritual life or death. For many who were motivated to stay and work for change, the decision was a claim that the church was women's as well as men's. For all women the turmoil and the toll have been exorbitant.

Some of the most creative work currently being done by feminist theologians is work on the topic of women and church. Rosemary Radford Ruether has envisioned "Women-Church," crying out,

> As Women-Church we claim the authentic mission of Christ, the true mission of the Church, the real agenda of our Mother-Father God who comes to restore and not to destroy our humanity, who comes to ransom the captives and to reclaim the earth as our Promised Land. We are not in exile, but the Church is in exodus with us. God's Shekinah, Holy Wisdom, the Mother-face of God has fled from the high thrones of patriarchy and has gone into exodus with us. She is with us as we flee from the smoking altars where women's bodies are sacrificed, as we cover our ears to blot out the inhuman voice that comes forth from the idol of patriarchy.[3]

Elisabeth Schüssler Fiorenza evokes the "*ekklesia* of women" as the setting in which women will "reclaim the right and

---

and Nelle Morton, "Women's Liberation and the Church," *Tempo*, 1 Oct. 1970.

3. Ruether, *Women-Church: Theology and Practice of Feminist Liturgical Communities* (San Francisco: Harper & Row, 1985), pp. 72-73.

power to articulate our own theology, to reclaim our own spirituality, and to determine our own and our sisters' religious life," in "solidarity with the most despised women suffering from the triple oppression of sexism, racism, and poverty."[4] Writing in a more reconstructive mode, Rebecca Chopp calls for the creation of a "community of emancipatory transformation."[5]

This collection of women's writings is a contribution to the creative work being done today on the topic of women and church. The unique contribution of this collection is rooted in the reality that these women write as active members of their own churches and as engaged participants in the ecumenical movement. Their writings bear witness to the solidarity that binds women across ecclesial chasms. This ecumenical solidarity among women, which deepens the challenge to the churches during this Ecumenical Decade of Churches in Solidarity with Women, is forged not only by what women have in common. Authentic solidarity is possible only as a predicate to the acknowledgment and appreciation of differences.

The initial impulse of the second wave of the women's movement was to assume that women's experience is the same. As we women named our own experience as distinct from men's experience, we advanced our commonality as a critique of the male-oriented order of things and as a complementary ticket for admission into their arenas. Slowly, as we have seen beyond inclusion to transformation, our eyes as well as our ears have been opened to the vast variety of our lives as women. We are blessed by richly diverse racial, cultural, and religious back-

4. Schüssler Fiorenza, "Women-Church: The Hermeneutical Center of Feminist Biblical Interpretation," in *Bread Not Stone: The Challenge of Feminist Biblical Interpretation* (Boston: Beacon Press, 1984), pp. 7, 8. See also Schüssler Fiorenza's *In Memory of Her: A Feminist Theological Reconstruction of Christian Origins* (New York: Crossroad, 1983), pp. 343-51.

5. See Chopp, *The Power to Speak: Feminism, Language, God* (New York: Crossroad, 1989), pp. 71-98.

grounds. We live, sometimes at our sisters' expense, in differing economic circumstances and at different places in the life cycle.

Recognizing our own differences has made manifest to us the challenge of appreciating differences around the world *without* sharply setting differences over against each other. For as we are coming to consciousness about our own differences, we begin to see that we live in a time when thinking in terms of sharp separations between self and other, subject and object, begets the tragedy of our world today. We are challenged to convert our energy for isolated causes into committed engagement with others. We are challenged by our own experience of one another to learn to live in ways that recognize and respect differences—indeed, receive differences as gifts—for the sake of life together. Churches, particularly during the Ecumenical Decade, are challenged to receive differences as the prerequisite for solidarity.

This collection is carefully crafted *not* to constrain its voices by conformity. The writings bear witness to the diverse experiences, perspectives, and commitments of the women. Unique strategies and styles are manifest throughout the volume. These differences at once point to the challenge of solidarity and offer the possibility for solidarity's realization.

Woven into this texture of differences are certain common themes. Three in particular are noteworthy. First, many of the women write about *ministry*. The common concern is not first and foremost the ordination of women but the nature of ministry. Questions about current perspectives on and practices of ministry are raised from various vantage points. Some find ministry too often features managerial manners. Some speak about the sheer impossibility of any one person fulfilling all the expectations of professional pastoral ministry. Many critique the hierarchical ordering of ministry and the way in which ministerial office sets priests and pastors apart from the people. Many wonder how the ordered ministry is related to the ministry of all baptized members of the church. These women are clearly more committed to new models of ministry than to participation in the practice of ministry prevalent in churches today.

A second emphasis related to these matters of ministry is evident in the repeated concern about authority and its abuse in the church. Again and again, the women speak about the way in which authority and power are confused in the church. This confusion is connected to the use and abuse of power over others in patriarchal structures. These women are seeking perspectives on power that move toward mutual empowerment, aware that this must be accompanied by thoroughgoing theological reconceptions of God and humanity.

Finally, the way in which the predominant language of the church renders women's presence as absence is again and again addressed by these women. Words are a matter of much concern. There is near unanimity that until the language of the church changes, there cannot be the radical renewal of the church being called for during the Ecumenical Decade. Without words that recognize differences, the challenge of solidarity will remain.

This collection, in short, is a discourse *of*—not *about*—differences and is dedicated to the challenge of solidarity. It is divided into three sections. In the first section, women from various ecclesial backgrounds have written in response to the question "As a woman in ministry, what are you wrestling with in your ecclesial context?" These women were asked to translate their challenges into challenges for the church. In the second section, women were asked to write on critical matters in the ecumenical movement. In the third section, women were asked to write toward a new ecumenical movement. Three of the four women contributing to this section live outside the United States and extend the vision of this collection to concern for solidarity with sisters across the continents.

The questions raised by this collection are not new. But this chorus of voices makes the questions increasingly insistent as women make connections between their own circumstances and the circumstances of our earth and all God's people. As the promise of progress unravels all around us, as we ourselves struggle in an age of alienation, this testament of courage and commitment offers hope that we stand on the threshold of transformation.

I   WOMEN AND CHURCH

Women in Evangelicalism and Pentecostalism

Edith L. Blumhofer

EVANGELICALS and pentecostals, like other Christians, have long wrangled over biblical passages that refer to female/male relationships in the church. Agreed only on their acceptance of biblical authority, they accuse one another of misunderstanding Scripture and succumbing to cultural influence. Bereft of a unified past and beset by deeply rooted differences, evangelicals and pentecostals recently have simply reacted to social changes related to the role of women rather than searching for a response faithful to their own inheritance.

A century ago, when the expectation of Christ's imminent return and excitement about an end-time effusion of the Holy Spirit illumined evangelical and pentecostal horizons, women were accepted as evangelists, missionaries, and voluntary association leaders. Despite feminists who deplore the way in which women have been denied a public forum in the West, and

Edith L. Blumhofer, a Methodist, is Associate Professor of History at Wheaton College in Wheaton, Illinois. She is a liaison to the NCC's Commission on Faith and Order, representing the Society of Pentecostal Studies, and is the author of The Assemblies of God: A Chapter in the Story of American Pentecostalism.

despite nagging notions about a "woman's sphere," many women in many evangelical and pentecostal traditions once managed to ignore the boundaries with considerable frequency. Although women's cultural authority in these religious movements has always been significant, women's institutional roles have steadily diminished during the past century. This decline, which corresponds to the experience of women in the wider culture, has enabled contemporary evangelicals to forget the significant roles women once played in their movements.

The contemporary discussion of women's place in the church emerged out of the shifting cultural norms of the post–World War II era. Like most other Americans before World War II, evangelicals and pentecostals regarded marriage as a matter of social utility and divorce as a matter of grave social concern. But as social values changed during the postwar years, as personal fulfillment replaced social utility as the foundation for marriage, traditional notions of social order advocated by evangelical leaders were out of touch with new realities. Fresh terms entered the evangelical discussion of "the woman question" as a yearning for order grew stronger as apparent cultural disorder surfaced.

Moreover, as the "battle for the Bible" intensified, some leaders were determined to marshall evangelical energies, backed by biblical authority, to strengthen their refusal to rethink their position on women's issues. With renewed passion these evangelical leaders evoked the hierarchical paradigm marked by male headship over women. Women as well as men were attracted to this model. The extent of the paradigm's popularity is evidenced by the volume of sales of a spate of publications about marriage issuing from evangelical and Pentecostal presses beginning in the 1960s. Tim and Beverly LaHaye, Bill Gothard, Larry Christenson, and Elisabeth Elliot are among the host of advocates for the view that woman is subordinate to man, according to the order of creation.

Recently, responding to the prods of secular feminism and

to the changing position of women in mainstream churches, a growing number of evangelicals have refused the hierarchical terms of discussion. They have posed new questions that disregard older assumptions about "true womanhood" or gender spheres. Adamantly affirming that "in Christ, all are one," they advocate the recognition of women as persons and criticize the segregated pattern of traditional "woman's work" in evangelical circles. Emerging evangelical biblical scholarship supports a partnership paradigm rather than the hierarchical paradigm of the past.

The growing number of evangelical women enrolled in seminaries are challenging more and more congregations, churches, and their institutions to deal practically—rather than theoretically—with "the woman question." The long list of contemporary public questions that focus on the family further complicate the already difficult discussion between proponents of the hierarchical paradigm for male/female relationships and proponents of the partnership paradigm.

There are several practical tasks among the challenges facing evangelicals and pentecostals in their attempt to affirm women and men through appeal to the Bible. I will briefly identify five of these tasks.

The first task is to learn about roles women have played in the past of the multifaceted evangelical and pentecostal traditions. It is clear that, numerically speaking, women have dominated evangelical congregations. Even a casual glance at hymnals, tracts, periodicals, and other evangelical literature attests to women's extensive contribution to the formation of evangelical spirituality.

Writing inclusive histories of evangelical and pentecostal traditions will be an essential second task that will facilitate this learning. A foray into evangelical history will not only reveal women's powerful presence in the church. It will also yield an awareness of the relationship between evangelical social agenda and evangelical attitudes about women. Nineteenth-century evangelicalism, for example, nurtured feminism within a frame-work of broad social sensitivity. Feminist concerns are part of a wider consideration of the social dimensions of evangelicalism and are to be addressed in this context.

A third task is the challenge of coming to terms with what is currently happening with regard to women's roles in the world and the church, as well as in biblical and theological studies. Social and economic realities compel women to enter the work force and therefore to reconsider traditional family roles. Women in seminaries seek opportunities to exercise their gifts and their calling to ministry. Evangelical feminists demonstrate that the arguments for the hierarchical paradigm are riddled with incon-sistencies and call evangelicals and pentecostals to be honest.

Additional pressures are coming to bear on pentecostals. It has become commonplace to assert that pentecostals—at least before 1920 or so—heartily endorsed women as ministers. Evangelical feminists suspect that pentecostal women are more affirmed by their churches. And pentecostal women, who in-sist on the inaccuracy of this suspicion, blame the influence of evangelicalism for the diminished role pentecostal women play. All of this is only partly true, however, because pentecostals have always had reservations about women who departed from their "proper sphere." Like their evangelical contempo-raries, pentecostals authenticated the witness of "prophesying daughters." But they also usually denied women any institu-tional presence. Pentecostal women flourished as evangelists and missionaries, but not as pastors or denominational leaders. They enjoyed cultural authority but had no institutional voice.

Today few pentecostal churches ordain women as pastors. In those churches that do—as in other evangelical and main-line churches—ordination has not resulted in equal access to the positions of leadership traditionally available to clergy. Prominent pentecostal and charismatic leaders have objected to women in authority as unequivocally as any other opponents of women ministers.

A fourth task is to grapple with issues raised by evangelical language, both formal and informal. Sensitivity to the changing use of language in the broader culture must increasingly inform the evangelical and pentecostal traditions. Many evangelicals and pentecostals reject gender-inclusive language for God. But this rejection need not render unimportant the choice of pronouns used to refer to human beings in sermons and songs. Since the 1920s, when evangelical leaders began to replace earlier celebrations of women "fellow laborers" with delineations of women's limitations, prominent evangelical leaders have called for reconceiving Christian life in ways that identify faith with masculine rather than feminine traits. Today evangelical and pentecostal congregations continue to depend on the prodigious efforts of women, women whose presence is absence according to the overwhelmingly masculine language of sermons, prayers, and songs.

Finally, there is the task of considering the role of women in church life with reference to the rights of laity in local congregations. In some evangelical churches, for example, women can be ordained but cannot be elected to church boards. Far-reaching institutional gains for women can come only as the basic issue of their identity as baptized Christian believers in relationship with other baptized believers in local congregations is clarified and confirmed. Denominational and institutional decisions cannot effectively meet contemporary challenges without the grass roots grappling to embody believers' oneness in Christ.

These and other issues raised in recent years by women seeking a more active role in churches, and by women and men striving to realize the fullness of a Christian understanding of personhood, challenge evangelicals and pentecostals to reassess and restructure another dimension of their calling to minister to and within the contemporary culture.

On Remembering What Is Impossible to Forget

Rita Nakashima Brock

THE political activism of the late 1960s inextricably linked the personal and political dimensions of life in ways that were empowering and transforming for me. As I became aware of sexism, I also became aware of racism against Japanese Americans. In that activist context, I was compelled to face for the first time the particularities of my life, which I had spent years trying to forget. These particularities marked me as different from others in the worlds of Kansas, Mississippi, and Germany, where I spent my childhood and adolescence. My awareness of my own complex identity was a tenuous insight deeply locked in my memory and easily buried by external demands.

When I awakened to feminism, I could not have predicted its impact on my particular church, the Christian Church (Disciples of Christ), the church I joined about twenty years ago.[1]

---

1. I spent the first six years of my life in a Japanese Buddhist family. By

Rita Nakashima Brock teaches in the Endowed Chair in the Humanities at Hamline University, St. Paul, Minnesota. She is the author of Journeys by Heart: A Christology of Erotic Power.

My struggle to remember what I have tried to forget has not been easy within the context of my church. I wrestle with how to stay in my church, since it often fails to touch what lies deepest in my heart. I am troubled by so much that marks my experience of the church: overwhelming whiteness; insensitivity to Asians; sexist language; homophobia; an often hollow spirituality; lack of prophetic courage. The deepening of my own spirituality has come not from the church but from feminist spirituality groups. Challenges to my own classism, heterosexism, and racism have likewise come from feminists and people of color often outside the context of the church. These women and men have supported me as I have confronted my own oppression of others. They have empowered me as a woman and as an Asian American by making race, gender, and other particularities of our identities matters of central concern.

My political struggles with the church have led me as a theologian to examine the way we understand our relationships to each other. I have a growing sense that the models for relationships in community that the church has offered us— models of self-sacrifice, servanthood, and harmonious/homogeneous unity—are neither healthy nor viable. I suspect that these models are in many ways models of exploitative and abusive relationships. I am convinced that the church often functions as a substitute family for many persons from dysfunctional families. What concerns me is that, while the image of the traditional patriarchal family put forward in the church may comfort some who come from dysfunctional families, there is little evidence that this image empowers change and liberation. Indeed, dysfunctional behavior is too often blessed by the church and covered over by theological words of love.

---

the time I joined the Disciples, I was a lapsed fundamentalist Baptist, lapsed because of my disillusionment with the intellectual narrowness of Baptists. The Christian Church (Disciples of Christ) is an ecumenically oriented, biblically based, predominantly white, mainline Protestant church with a congregational polity.

My feminist work with sexual and domestic violence and co-dependency has helped me to see my own behaviors more clearly and to heal some of my own suffering. I have begun to see destructive patterns embedded in my church's life. We are often psychologically unprepared to deal with honest criticism or with passionate feelings, especially sexual feelings and anger. We often operate by avoidance and appeasement. Personal integrity and honesty are replaced by the desire for admiration and approval, exhibited as we abandon ourselves to the needs of others or as we strive for success at the expense of listening to our own feelings and nurturing ourselves. Control becomes manipulatively manifest in paternalistic benevolence or in the need to change the behavior of others.[2] We also find it difficult to understand our own role in oppressing others and to affirm the human differences among us. As I examine these psychological dimensions of the church's pattern of co-dependency, I begin to understand their powerful political consequences as well as their profound entrenchment. Changing these patterns will be extremely difficult.

Skirmishes for control of theology, policy, and practice have become commonplace at our national church assemblies. Fundamentalists are digging in their heels against entering the modern era. They are determined not only to hold their ground but also to push the church back to a hierarchically ordered time and space in which God the Father in heaven judges all and the Bible is the supreme authority. A nostalgic past is their haven. Progressives want to usher the church into a postmodern twenty-first century. They see that during the twenty-first century the church will be called to understand a world of relativity

2. See Harriett G. Lerner, *The Dance of Anger: A Woman's Guide to Changing the Patterns of Intimate Relationships* (New York: Harper & Row, 1985); Alice Miller, *Thou Shalt Not Be Aware: Psychoanalysis and Society's Betrayal of the Child,* trans. Hunter and Hildegarde Hannum (New York: Farrar, Straus & Giroux, 1984); and Anne Wilson Schaef, *When Society Becomes an Addict* (New York: Harper & Row, 1987).

and constant change, to reverse the widening gap between rich and poor, to heal communities torn by racism, war, and totalitarianism, to reconceive the place of human beings in our interdependent ecology, to formulate nonpatriarchal theologies, and to humanize families, as well as to empower changes in women's status. For the most radical progressives, the church is moving much too slowly in response to these matters.

Although fundamentalists and progressives differ dramatically in their diagnosis of the church's sickness and on what would restore its health, both are focused on changing the church. Moderates, caught in the middle, appear to believe in a benignly paternalistic God and adhere to friendly tolerance. In such a situation, solidarity seems all but impossible, because solidarity is forged from honest confrontation and mutual confidence amid struggle.

Our church doesn't know how to be a healthy community. We act like a dysfunctional family. I struggle with my anger as I search for ways to say what is passionately important to me to others whose views seem starkly opposed to mine. It is hard for me to listen to them. But I know I am a more effective agent of change when I focus on the clarity of my own vision rather than focusing on changing the behavior of others. In my own clarity I find peace, joy, and empowerment.

I, a radical feminist woman of color, stay in the church because, as I confront the meaning of my personal identity, my faith, and my longing for community, I do not find it helpful to limit my options to being in or out of the church. I have met members of the church who share many of my concerns for justice. They have nurtured and encouraged me even when they did not agree with every conviction I held. Moreover, I refuse to surrender the church to those who want me out of it. The church belongs to no one group but to all God's people baptized into Jesus Christ. Ultimately, it is the church of all its members, not just its leaders and theologians; it belongs to God. My commitment to the transformation of the church makes me as central to its life as those who want to preserve the church as it has been in the past.

The clearer I am about my own identity and culture, the clearer I am that I am neither in nor out of the church but work surrounded by my own integrity amid the complex range of my relationships. The range of my relationships reaches across boundaries of nation, race, class, gender, age, and church structure. I am particularly strengthened for my struggle within the church by my global sisters. From them I know that in some Asian, Latin American, and African countries, the church is at the forefront of movements for liberation of oppressed people. I am strengthened as I remember that my church, like me, has changed considerably in the last twenty years. As I experience solidarity across denominational lines with more feminists and people of color who are challenging the church, it is easier to remember—and to persevere.

Hispanic Women in the Roman Catholic Church

Ada Maria Isasi-Diaz

A HEADLINE in the *New York Times* read, "Switch by Hispanic Catholics Changes Face of U.S. Religion." The article underneath said that "perhaps four million of the 20 million Hispanic Americans" have left the Roman Catholic
Church for Protestant Christianity. According to Andrew Gree-
ley, who was quoted in the article, 23 percent of all Hispanic
Americans are Protestants, and 60,000 are joining Protestant
churches each year. The Roman Catholic bishop and two priests
quoted in the article gave several reasons for this mass exodus
of Hispanics from the Roman Catholic Church: the lack of
priests; the lack of outreach into Hispanic communities; the
bureaucratic and impersonal nature of parish structures; the

---

*Ada Maria Isasi-Diaz, a Catholic, was born and raised in La Habana,
Cuba. She is Associate General Director of Church Women United.
Currently she teaches at New York Theological Seminary and is working
to develop a theology from the perspective of Hispanic women. She is
the author, with Yolanda Taranga, of* Hispanic Women: Prophetic
Voice in the Church.

increasingly rationalistic and moralistic character of American Catholicism.[1]

These reasons—with which I agree—tell me that those in positions of power in the institutional structures of the Roman Catholic Church must look at the understanding of ministry, the way ministry is structured, and the priorities for ministry prevalent in the Roman Catholic Church. Church authorities must also examine which church teachings are being emphasized and how those teachings are being interpreted and presented. They must undertake these considerations aware of the fact that Hispanics are the largest racial/ethnic group in the church today, and that by the turn of the century Hispanics will constitute over 50 percent of the Roman Catholic Church in the United States. An appropriate response to this fact will involve changing the hierarchy of the church. Presently, less than 10 percent of the bishops are Hispanics. An appropriate response will also mean accepting the religious understandings and practices that Hispanics revere rather than considering them to be curiosities.

The fact that there is little ministry among Hispanics is often attributed to the small number of Hispanic priests. But no mention is made of the fact that church authorities will not ordain large numbers of Hispanic Roman Catholics who feel called to priestly ministry: Hispanic women and married Hispanic men. Instead, authorities merely make one more appeal for us to pray for vocations. Embedded in this appeal is what Edward Schillebeeckx has called "an ideological element." Schillebeeckx says, "No Christian would deny the value and force of prayer, even for vocations; but if the reason for the shortage of priests is 'church legislation' which can be changed and modified in the course of time for pastoral reasons, then a

1. Roberto Suro, "Switch by Hispanic Catholics Changes Face of U.S. Religion," *New York Times*, 14 May 1989.

call to prayer can act as an excuse; in other words, it can be a reason for not changing this law."[2]

The Roman Catholic Church continues to subscribe to what Schillebeeckx calls the "ontological sacerdotalist view of ministry."[3] This view of ministry often sets priests apart from the people, since priestly functions are reduced to celebrating the sacraments and sustaining church structures. This view of ministry may flourish among people of the dominant culture, since societal structures have been established for their benefit. But among any oppressed and marginalized people, the church and thus its ministers must accompany the people in their struggle for liberation. Only as church authorities come to understand the close connection between salvation and liberation will they be able to view ministry as "an ecclesial function within the community."[4]

I think that such an understanding of ministry should be operative among Hispanics not only in the Roman Catholic Church but also in all Christian churches. Ministry exercised as "an ecclesial function within the community" may vary according to the different church traditions to which a particular sector of the Hispanic community relates. But ministry as an ecclesial function within the Hispanic community should always be shaped by the community and its struggle for liberation.

This cannot happen unless the Roman Catholic Church and the Protestant churches know and appreciate the religious understandings and practices of the Hispanic community. For, even though most Hispanics are Roman Catholics, Hispanic Catholicism does not necessarily have "official" Catholicism as its primary point of reference. Our Catholicism is quite distinc-

2. Schillebeeckx, *Ministry—Leadership in the Community of Jesus Christ* (New York: Crossroad, 1981), p. 94.

3. Ibid., p. 70.

4. Ibid.

tive because of the way in which it was brought to and established in our countries of origin. Roman Catholicism came to
Latin America and the Caribbean with the *conquista;* it was an
intrinsic part of the conquering culture. Damage wrought by
the *conquista* included the devastation of the religious world of
the conquered in addition to political and economic enslavement.

Christianity, as an integral element of the conquering culture, was imposed and also played a critical role as moral justifier
of the *conquista.* Real inculturation—"the process of making
personal the traditional culture of the society," in other words,
the society of the *conquistadores*[5]—did not take place because
education was not made available to the majority of the popu-
lation. Instead, there was a "culturization" of Roman Catholicism. Roman Catholicism became culture, and it has become a
cultural expression.[6] This explains why the beliefs and practices
of the *conquistadores* are today integral not only to Hispanic
Catholicism but also to Hispanic culture.

Another integral aspect of our Catholicism and Hispanic
culture is the religious beliefs, traditions, and practices of Amer-
indian and African religions. Elements from these religions have
been fused with those of Catholicism to form the religious
"system of symbols" that creates what Clifford Geertz calls
"powerful, pervasive, and long-lasting moods and motivations"
for Hispanics.[7] Although different religious traditions raise their
voices in strong objection to such fusion of elements, no religious tradition is exempt from some syncretism, the organic
process that occurs when different cultures with different religions meet.

Today, Protestant denominations with a ministry among
Hispanics as well as the Roman Catholic Church need to re-

5. Paulo Agirrebaltzategi, *Configuracion eclesial de las culturas* (Bilbao,
Spain: Universidad de Deusto, 1976), p. 82.
6. Ibid.
7. Geertz, *Interpretation of Cultures* (New York: Basic Books, 1973), p. 90.

spect all elements of Hispanic Catholicism that are an intrinsic part of Hispanic culture. Such things as devotion to the saints, outward expressions of faith in processions and the use of candles, and the centrality of devotion to Mary cannot be changed or ignored without doing violence to Hispanic culture.

As I talk with Hispanic women, I realize that their religious and church experiences are indeed ecumenical. Maria, for example, tells me that she attends a Protestant church. But she also tells me she will have her daughter baptized in the Roman Catholic Church "because I am still a Catholic." Margarita is a Catholic who goes to mass weekly. "But I also go to other churches with my friends," she adds. These and other Hispanic women are most comfortable recognizing diverse manifestations of the divine as well as diverse expressions of the relationship between human beings and the divine. Their functional religious pluralism moves beyond traditional doctrinal purity and emerges as religious solidarity, which becomes a source of their motivation, strength, and strategies in their struggle for liberation.

Ministry as an ecclesial function within the Hispanic community is confronted with the challenge of this liberation-focused, functional religious pluralism. Ministry within the Hispanic community will be effective only when Protestant churches and the Roman Catholic Church recognize and respect this functional religious pluralism. This will happen only when they embrace the religious practices and beliefs that are an integral part of Hispanic culture.

Reformed—and Always Reforming?

Aurelia T. Fule

IT would be hard to say what hurts women more—the church's separation from human reality or from divine reality. But it is fitting for me to speak about the way the separation hurts me most. While I do so by narrowing down to my church, the Presbyterian Church, U.S.A., my story is not without relevance to other churches. Before I tell my tale, focusing on the matter of our language, I will briefly introduce my tradition.

The roots of all Presbyterian and Reformed churches in the United States and in other countries go back to the day of Pentecost, through Geneva's great reformer: John Calvin. Those who are Presbyterian also trace our tradition through the teaching of the Scotsman John Knox and the Westminster divines. Moving out in mission during the nineteenth century, we made converts throughout the world. Today there are more members

---

Aurelia T. Fule was educated in her native Hungary as well as in Britain and the United States. She is Associate for Faith and Order in the Theology and Worship Unit of the Presbyterian Church, U.S.A., headquartered in Louisville, Kentucky. She is a member of the NCC's Commission on Faith and Order and of its Executive Committee.

of Presbyterian and Reformed churches in South Asia than in Europe and North America.

Most of the teachings of my church are those of the church catholic. Our re-formation resulted in at least two significant shifts in theological understanding: Scripture is given more authority than tradition, and salvation is understood to be by God's grace alone, through faith. This has led Presbyterians to stress the sovereignty of God more than many other churches do. We long for genuine piety in our life, remembering that Calvin considered his formative work, *The Institutes of the Christian Religion*, to be not a "summa theologiae" according to the custom of his day, but a "summa pietatis," the sum of piety. We cherish the church as a corporate and committed body whose government is theologically informed and intended to involve the whole people of God through elected representatives. We are, therefore, a church that is non-clerically governed. We believe that Christian calling includes responsibilities for transforming society and witnessing in the world. We are committed to the ecumenical movement, understanding ourselves to be part of the true church, not the whole true church.

Perhaps we are particularly distinguished by our conviction that individual as well as corporate Christian life is a journey, not an arrival. So we speak of ourselves as reformed and still "semper reformanda," always reforming or being reformed. This predisposition to ongoing reformation is evidenced by the number of Reformed confessions that have been written through the centuries. These confessions bear witness to our conviction that new truths may be seen in Scripture and that the Spirit may lead in new ways.

Most Presbyterian and Reformed churches today have taken this ongoing reformation to heart in relation to the role of women in the church, confirming God's call to women and men to all forms of ministry. This has included the willingness to ordain women as well as men to the ministry of the Word.

Many churches of my tradition have even stopped speaking about the whole people of God as "brethren" and "sons of God."

But questions remain. Have Presbyterian and Reformed churches really been reformed with regard to the role of women? Are we who belong to these churches really in solidarity with women? If we think we are, then it seems to me that there is a significant split between our perception and reality. We Presbyterian and Reformed church members tend to think of ourselves as members of well-educated, middle-class, mainline communities living in traditional families. In reality, however, we use ninth-grade language in our publications, and many of our members come from the ranks of the divorced, single parents, working mothers, the unemployed, and the poor.

At home, when I have my glasses on and I look in the mirror sometimes where the light is brighter than it is over my dressing table, I am amazed that I have wrinkles and, worse, that my skin is no longer tight. I know I am middle-aged and my husband and I have grown children, but my image of myself is informed by the shape of my head and the bones of my face more than by my aging skin. What was is still in my mind. Is this what informs the self-perception of Presbyterian and Reformed churches as well? And, given the fact that the churches have a longer history than my own, is there a greater difference between self-perception and present reality for the churches than for me? If my image of myself is as I was 15 or 20 years ago, is the churches' image of themselves as they were 40 or 50 years ago? When will we catch up with contemporary circumstances?

Between 1905 and 1966, the Presbyterian Church, U.S.A., opened all ordained offices to women. More recently, by an act of the highest governing body, the church's official language about God and God's people is to be inclusive. But most language of theology and worship remains as it was. Moreover, the debate over whether or not faithfulness to Scripture requires that we speak of God in the masculine gender continues. I am convinced that until our language is truly transformed to include the image of women for human and divine reality, my church will not be in solidarity with women. I go farther: unless we move from this place, God—who transcends all our metaphors and similes—will not be known by us, because we are blocking our own perception of the divine self and the divine will. If we believe we have arrived and are no longer traveling toward the truth, we have become un-formable in God's hands and unteachable in our hearts. More than four hundred years ago, Calvin said that to know God is the justification and end of human existence. This is still true today.

We bear within us an innate knowledge of God whose wholeness is unmarred by present language patterns. I learned this from my daughter, Susan. When she was a third grader, she came home from vacation Bible school chanting a verse she had memorized: "This is what God is like. Love him, obey him, follow his will." Every lesson ended with these words, so she repeated the refrain daily. One afternoon I mentioned that she always referred to God by using "he," "him," and "his." Susan replied, "That's how you talk about God." In my mind I suddenly saw Peter, her older brother, who she thought was all-knowing and who in her heart was all-loved. "Do you think God is more like Peter than you?" I asked. Almost instantly she answered, "More like both of us."

This precious innate knowledge of God is de-formed by the language with which we are taught theology, with which we worship. We still do not hear Genesis 1:27: "God created . . . in the image of God . . . male and female." Both of us, women and men, are indeed in the image of God.

Our worlds—personal, ecclesial, ecumenical, social—would be transformed if we would move from traditional theological metaphors and titles such as "Lord," "King," and "Father" to new metaphors that are life-giving for all God's people—metaphors that await us in the Scripture to which my particular people, Presbyterian and Reformed, have regularly turned for re-formation of our faith and life. Phyllis Trible has long since called our attention to some of these metaphors that are at once new and ancient. She speaks, for example, about "the Hebrew root, *rhm,* which in the singular form *(rechem)* is 'womb' and in the plural *(rachamim)* 'compassion,'" tracing the journey of this Hebrew root from the womb of women to the compassion of God. "This metaphor . . . with persistence and power," she clarifies, "saturates the Bible." Moreover, she points to "other passages [that] join this journey to depict Yahweh poetically as a deity who conceives, who is pregnant, who writhes in labor pains, who brings forth a child and nurses it."[1]

For women, for children, for the voiceless, for the poor, for men, for all who ask for compassion, can a new name for God be "Compassion"? The journey toward the compassionate God—who seeks rather than rules, who gently leads rather than commands—is the journey of being continually re-formed. It is a journey of solidarity with women among all God's people. Will the church set forth on such a journey?

1. Transcript of remarks made at a symposium held in New York on 8 Dec. 1977. See also Phyllis Trible, *God and the Rhetoric of Sexuality,* ed. Walter Brueggemann and John R. Donahue, no. 20 in the Overtures to Biblical Theology Series (Philadelphia: Fortress Press, 1978).

". . . And Then Turn South . . ."

Lauree Hersch Meyer

I GREW up in rural Virginia, where directions for getting from here to there were given with clues from the landscape, the geographical reality of the region. Whether you were traveling by path, road, or just "following your nose," the steady modulation of field to farm to village matched the rhythmic undulation of forest to field to stream.

Then my job led me to six midwest states east of the Mississippi where I traveled by car. A stranger to the area, I frequently asked directions. Not only was the flat openness new to me; the willing guidance and warm hospitality with which directions were offered came to me in a foreign language: "Drive another mile east, and then turn south for two miles; it'll be right there on the corner."

Today when I inquire about the location of vibrant faith in

Lauree Hersch Meyer is Associate Professor of Biblical Theology and Interpretation at Bethany Theological Seminary, the graduate school of theology of the Church of the Brethren in Oak Brook, Illinois. She is a member of the NCC's Commission on Faith and Order and of its Executive Committee.

23

the congregation where I worship, the seminary where I teach, and the denomination into which I was born, I find myself again a stranger to the directions. Once more I am vocationally placed in a landscape where others' directions disorient me. This time, the directions given to me seem to address a landscape as different from the one I see as the tangled web that guided travel in cozy rural Virginia was different from the starkly geometric lines on midwestern grids.

The significance of this change is deeper than geography. I participate in conversations about seminary, national offices, congregations, and church "crises" that deeply matter to me: shrinking funds and leadership; a membership hard-pressed to support our programs and institutions; concerned voices of those with limited economic resources, unfamiliar customs, and different values. Thus peoples such as Native Americans, African-Americans, Hispanics, Asians, and women assume that church membership means access to decision-making and leadership as well as self-expression and enrollment into current structures and programs; yet they see no evidence to support their assumption. Similarly, in academic life there are diverse ethnic and Third World peoples who have no Anglo-American academic skills, understandings, methods, or data, and who lead seminaries to puzzle out how to graduate these students who, willy-nilly, *are* leaders of the emerging church and, at the same time, how to meet degree standards established by the American Theological Society.

The directions that long-standing leaders of the church offer for negotiating this shifting landscape disorient me. Can the tired, established-becoming-disestablished churches of the North engage the energetic, emerging Two-Thirds' World churches of the South and the East as our sisters and brothers? How will we relate with these peoples made not in our Euro-American image but uniquely in God's image?

The job descriptions of presidents of seminaries, heads of communion, and even pastors increasingly suggest that search committees are looking for individuals with the managerial skills to run institutions and the public relations savvy to fund them. The presupposition of these job descriptions is that the church resides in institutions, a presupposition that renders its mission and its meaning secondary. Curricular decisions are converted to educational program objectives and assigned to deans. Ecclesial matters are reconfigured as structural, political, and policy agenda assigned to middle management.

I wrestle with how to respond to the directions for churchly faith and practice that arise from this *understanding* of the landscape. The nature of Christian leaders seems secondary in contemporary ecclesial life. It is as if we Euro-American "elders" fear we will lose control of the right to set the terms for ecclesial and academic life and structures. But we "elders," who see the world awash in changes we can neither manage nor control, must choose how to interpret the changes. Will we interpret them as crises that threaten to erode our possessions and inheritance? Or will we interpret the changes as evidence that the superabundant love of God reaches and restores inheritance to those whom our hearts abandon without compassion?

As I understand it, Christian leaders are called to live fundamentally from doxology that renews and re-aligns our hearts toward God, so *all* who live in Christ become images of and way markers to the source of life. As I understand it, although church members manage and control legal power in political, economic, and ecclesial structures, our religious inheritance calls us to use power toward fulfillment that is manifest in God's promise that in *each* people of faith, *all* peoples are blessed. When strangers enter our landscape and ask for directions to locate the risen Christ today, what will we say?

My answer is, "Turn south . . ." Turn south, where the rediscovery of spiritual joy in Latin American base communities is deeper than economic poverty or death. Turn south, where the vibrant energy of young African churches is bonding with the legacy of colorful tribal buoyance. Turn east, where Orthodox, who distinguish Christianity from success, sanctify their world by identifying the image of God's holiness in all life about them. Turn southeast, where the church *of* as well as *in* Asia incarnates its faith as a Christian minority in daily intercourse with other peoples of faith.

All who worship and bless God are commissioned to live as members of God's family, blessing one another in God's name. In global perspective, what we First World Christians call crisis often discloses a long-honored idolatry. We too readily assume that the social form and cultural images of our God-given promise and blessing are normative for all of God's people. When our basic loyalty and identity are rooted in structures of legal justice and economic power, we children of God act as owners who possess an inheritance that we may bestow on others according to laws of justice and righteousness we control. Who is the prodigal when we who hold power view a feast as wasted or as prepared for the wrong siblings? Who is lost when our hearts do not rejoice as the culturally and economically dispossessed are restored and celebrated?

Christian idolatry is a posture that subverts the gospel of Jesus Christ, treating salvation as a possession owned by the socially powerful who manage it and determine who shall be powerful by conferring office upon them. This attitude puts us at the center of "our" gospel. When "others" nevertheless receive whatever crumbs fall from our table, we rage when "they" enjoy what *we* do not bestow.

Scripture is a recital of God's dramatic renewal of the believing community through persons we good "elders" view as prodigals and prostitutes:

• Abram and Sarai, who "left home . . .";

• Tamar, Rahab, Bathsheba, Ruth, and Mary, whom Matthew remembers as transgressing sexual, national, and religious taboos to assure continuity in Israel's messianic lineage when its male bearers floundered;

- Joseph, who as a "righteous" man was about to put away his pregnant fiancée quietly when God called him to a far more controversial and costly righteousness: to bond his life and reputation to hers and adopt (into his messianic lineage) her socially and religiously illegitimate offspring;

- Moses and Paul, overachievers in three cultures who were at home in none until each found a way to offer to God his best in covenant for a whole people . . .

The story now names us. How will we interpret the "crisis" swirling about us? Who will we say is lost? What landscape directions will we give when asked where God is renewing creation in Christ's living body? My challenge to churches in the United States is to reassess the landscape. When asked for directions by persons seeking vibrant hearts in which the living Christ is at work, may we "elders" turn from fear that interprets change as crisis and join God's great feast to which all have been invited.

For our crisis, like our salvation, surfaces visibly when God prepares a feast for the prodigals and prostitutes we cast out. Yet God always calls each of us to bless one another, living together as offspring of God's redeeming and compassionate heart.

The Challenge of "Both/And" Theology

Mary E. Hunt

THE women-church movement in the United States, a network of feminist faith-sharing groups, holds together both a feminist critique of Christianity and a powerful experience of religious community. It is a way for women to "be church" without being oppressed by the churches. It blends sacraments and solidarity in a new combination of women-led worship and political action. This "both/and" approach is at once an accomplishment and a challenge for a movement that is scarcely a decade old. How long the tension can be maintained without losing its fine edge is my main concern as a theologian and a participant.

Two hundred or more women-church groups meet in the United States. Participants share a common concern for spir-

Mary E. Hunt is a Catholic feminist theologian. She is currently Co-Director of WATER, the Women's Alliance for Theology, Ethics, and Ritual in Silver Spring, Maryland. She is the editor of From Woman-Pain to Woman-Vision, *a collection of the writings of Anne McGrew Bennett, and author of the forthcoming* Fierce Tenderness: A Feminist Theology of Friendship.

itual searching as well as for the religious agency that patriarchal Christianity—especially Roman Catholicism, from which most women in these groups come—does not permit, much less promote.[1] Religious agency involves women naming our own experiences, women making decisions on the basis of our experiences so named, and women forming communities of accountability to be challenged to live with integrity.

In women-church groups the Eucharist is celebrated, Goddess chants are used, and myriad poems, readings, and songs enliven celebration. Pentecost is enjoyed with an emphasis on the diversity of modes of communication. The community of faith is the central focus. Above all, women's time, resources, and energies are redirected from patriarchal churches. These gifts are instead engaged in service with all marginalized people in the spirit of a "discipleship of equals" about which biblical scholar Elisabeth Schüssler Fiorenza has written.[2]

Much as I celebrate religious life in the women-church movement, and much as I recommend it to women who have come to the end of their patience with patriarchal religious life, I see three contradictions in the movement: ministry, money, and race. These contradictions are not at all unique to women-church; they have decisive implications for the whole Christian community. I will explore each of these as illustrations of how "both/and" approaches to being church are shaping our collective future.

I begin with ministry. The theo-politic of women-church is anticlerical. Women's experience of oppressive Roman Catholic clericalism, as well as their deep distrust of all hierarchy, clearly forms this theo-political posture. Moreover, many women see

1. "Women-church" is a word on the lips of more and more women in Protestant churches. As they work like "ecclesial termites" to make changes from within, they also participate in the movement of sisters for whom the only alternative to women-church is no church.

2. See Elisabeth Schüssler Fiorenza, *In Memory of Her: A Feminist Theological Reconstruction of Christian Origins* (New York: Crossroad, 1983).

the ordination of women in Protestant churches as a move that puts them above the laity, a move that flies in the face of any commitment to equality. Questions about models of ministry abound. Ministry is usually hard work with low pay, low prestige, and long hours—the all-too-familiar recipe for a job fit for a woman. The feminization of ministry seems to confirm this perception, because it puts women in relative positions of power at considerable cost.

And yet the women-church movement celebrated the consecration of Bishop Barbara Harris as the first female bishop in the Episcopal Church in the United States. Because we are ecumenical and because we applaud the religious agency of women in whatever ecclesial context, women-church friends happily say, "We have a bishop." Indeed, Bishop Harris represents an ecclesial achievement that many women, even Roman Catholic women, would imitate if we could have the chance. The challenge for the women-church movement is to let neither the anti-ordination position nor the pro-ordination position predominate, but to let the positions co-exist in mutual critique.

The second issue—money—confronts us with another challenge. Like all movements for the sake of structural change, women-church needs money to spread the good news of equality. Like most fledgling movements, women-church barely has a shirt on its back. It is dependent on the hospitality and largess of its friends, along with the creativity and cunning of its leaders.

In search of women-church support, women are diverting funds from mainline denominations. Some are following my fanciful suggestion that women take a little from the basket as the offering is taken to recollect the resources our mothers and grandmothers donated that were put to use for patriarchal purposes. But the real problem is not loose change; it is buildings, schools, publishing companies, and newspapers that belong to the Christian community and are not available to women-church.

We cannot have our cake and eat it too. We cannot accept money and favors from institutions which marginalize us and expect that we can do whatever we want with them. For example, one women-church group in Europe met in a church building until the parish council recognized that the church was better known for its women-church celebrations than for its regular worship services. The open door closed behind the group. The church will not pay for its own transformation, at least not knowingly.

Our "both/and" approach asks us to seek funds and favors from those friendly souls who have their hands on the purse strings of major denominations and, at the same time, to find ways to finance a movement that is fundamentally about substantive structural change of the churches. This means teaching people, particularly women, that religious life costs money, especially if we do not want to foster more of the volunteerism which so often has been unjust for women.

The third challenge that calls for "both/and" sorts of solutions is presented by the racial composition of the women-church movement. It is no secret that the movement was begun by predominantly white, middle-class women whose comparative privilege gave us the wherewithal to dare to be church differently. At the same time, we have always had a strong commitment to eradicating racism, both personal and structural. We have struggled, with the most modest success, to make our movement inclusive.

The contradiction in this regard is twofold. First, a movement is shaped from inception in ways that are determinative. Simply adding African-American, Hispanic, and Asian women to the movement on Anglo-American women's terms is unacceptable. This simple addition would merely assuage white women's conscience about inclusivity, not respond meaningfully to the integrity of women of color. Second, the religious experiences of African-American, Hispanic, and Asian women in this country are conditioned by the country's social, economic, and political circumstances. Women-church is not necessarily the best way for them to articulate their faith. In fact, it may be detrimental to their goals. For example, the achievement of African-American women in ministry, their historical "holy boldness" as religious agents in their own churches, as well as their need to forge strong family bonds with men mean that women-church is often a less than desirable option for them. Similar dynamics with different stories are told by Asian and Hispanic women.

Racism is, in my judgment, the most painful and difficult "both/and" challenge we confront. It is hard for white women to acknowledge that even the most valiant efforts at inclusivity are inadequate to address the "structural enemyhood"[3] which separates women from one another by drawing racial, ethnic, and class lines. The strategy I advise for women-church is to redouble our efforts to be inclusive and, at the same time, to encourage women of diverse racial/ethnic groups to be religious agents out of their own integrity in their own communities. Women-church can listen to and learn from these women whether or not they are participants in our movement. We can, for example, hear and heed the womanist work of African-American theologians such as Dolores Williams, Katie Geneva Cannon, and Cheryl Gilkes, work that is based not simply on the rights of women but on the very survival of women and dependent children.[4]

The way in which the women-church movement responds to these three challenges—ministry, money, and race—will be paradigmatic for how it will grow. To the extent that we overcome the "either/or" mentality predominant in patriarchal churches with "both/and" strategies committed to inclusivity and creativity without contradiction, we may be a way marker

3. Cf. Lois Kirkwood's doctoral dissertation, Union Theological Seminary, in which she details the concept of "structural enemyhood."

4. See Williams, "Womanist Theology: Black Women's Voices," *Christianity and Crisis*, 2 Mar. 1987, pp. 66-70.

for things to come in the whole church. We may be a sign that ministry may be shared, resources distributed equitably, and diverse races respected in their own integrity without domination. While these seem to be dreams, the continuing life of the women-church movement will be measured by whether or not we help these dreams come true.

Authority in the Church:
An Anglican Confession

Patricia Wilson-Kastner

AFTER fifteen years of full-time seminary teaching, first in
Minnesota and then in New York, I moved to Norwich,
Connecticut, to become rector of the Church of the Resurrection in February 1989. I wasn't fired from my teaching position.
I didn't tire of city living. I didn't even get bored with teaching
and going to faculty meetings. After years of devoting myself
primarily to instruction and participating part-time in parish
ministry, I decided it was time for total immersion in the parish.
I had long said I was convinced that the center of church life
was in the parish. It was time to practice my profession.

The Church of the Resurrection is a modest-sized parish.
We are proud of our enlightened Anglo-Catholic tradition,
with its strong sacramental, incarnational theology. We
struggle to know what this tradition means today. Ideally, the
church wants to be a worshipful community that is active in

---

*Patricia Wilson-Kastner is rector of the Church of the Resurrection in
Norwich, Connecticut, and a member of the Episcopal Church's Stand-
ing Committee on Ecumenical Relations. She is the author of* Faith,
Feminism, and the Christ *and* Imagery in Preaching.

the world. In reality, the church is in conflict. Some want the parish to be a safe, isolated haven in the face of a threatening world. Some want the parish to minister to the world, affirming the good in it. As a feminist theologian and former seminary professor, I had hoped for a more unusual or unmistakably contemporary conflict: conflict over inclusive language or the morality of working for the defense industry. Instead, I have discovered the more common and centuries-old conflict between church and world being waged in my parish.

And yet I sense that it is superficial to describe this conflict as a conflict over whether or not we are a self-contained church or risk ourselves in mission in the world. The deeper question, after all, is why we experience such a conflict. The gospel is clear about believers being sent forth in mission. Our very baptism is baptism into a church in mission. Why, then, is there such conflict in my parish over what we in the church are called to be and to do by virtue of our very existence?

As I address this question, I am struck by the awareness that we are struggling in our own context with a question that others are wrestling with around the globe: What is the authority of the church? I do not mean merely "What right do we have to do certain things rather than others?" but "What are the roots of our ability and our responsibility to act?" In New Testament terms, we are seeking not only our *exousia* but more fundamentally our *dunamis*.

What is the power, the might, the energy that constitutes us as a Christian community and consequently empowers us to carry out our mission, individually and corporately, as baptized Christians? We come to the church out of all sorts of motivations. Some of us come to be safe from change. Some of us come hoping we will find a place to belong. Some of us come with a sense of responsibility for the needs of our neighbors. An individual may be in a parish because it is the only place in his life where he feels important and valued. A priest

may be in a parish because of the sacralized power she has
over people, power that takes care of her need for control in
a hostile and alienating world. Not all of these motivations
which draw us to the church can lead us to the heart of the
church, to the divine source of Christian life. Some motivations leave us in the vestibule. If we are not led to the heart
of the church, our power will become distorted, idolatrous.
We will inevitably confuse the energy of *dunamis* with the
exercise of *exousia*.

This confusion is certainly evident in the Anglican communion as well as in the wider Christian world. We Anglicans
are analyzing our cultural diversity, our inability to let go of
legalistic decision-making devices ("What do the canons/
rubrics say?"), our divergent understandings of what fidelity to
the tradition of the church means today. As a woman priest I
have problems in the Anglican communion, since many prov-
inces refuse to recognize my ordination. The Archbishop of
Canterbury has argued against accepting the validity of my duly
conferred American Episcopal ordination on the grounds of
English canon law! African Anglican priests argue against the
ordination of African women on the grounds that women are
not fit for ministry at the altar if they can be bought and sold
in marriage, never questioning the latter custom! This ferment
directs us to the fundamental difficulty: the distortion and
idolatry of power that we experience in the church.

A brief but vital essay entitled "The Authority of Love" by
Edward W. Scott, former Anglican Primate of Canada, has
helped me see beyond our contemporary circumstance. Scott
notes that the New Testament distinguishes between power and
authority as rooted in God and power and authority as rooted
in the world of human decision-making. He is convinced that
we Anglicans will be able to resolve our conflicts and concerns
about authority and actions only when we are able to center
ourselves in the power rooted in God, who is love. When we
root ourselves in God, who is love, we will become a "loving,

supporting, challenging community" able to be a channel of God's love into the world.[1]

My own experience and struggle suggest that Archbishop Scott has identified the fundamental issue in our attempts to be the church. Unless we are grounded in the life of God, who is unbounded and all-encompassing love, we cannot be the church. We might be a comforting community, an occasional political force, an arena in which to act out unhealthy and co-dependent relationships, a well-ordered group that performs aesthetically pleasing rituals. But we will not be the church— the gracious, imperfect yet faithful continuation of the Incarnation in the world. We will not be the church where, in response to God's call, we celebrate the death and resurrection of Jesus and are empowered by the Spirit to be agents of reconciliation in the world.

I think that the issue of authority confronting the church is at once quite simple and tremendously challenging. It involves changing hierarchical tradition. It involves changing the image of a monarchical God governing a people who must "be good." We are called to be radically faithful to the love of God made manifest to us in Jesus Christ and poured into our hearts by the Holy Spirit. We each and all are called to live in intimate communion with God. We are called to live with God as the center and ground of our lives, as the source and standard of all our actions. If we so live, we will be Christ's holy catholic church. We will be free to risk ourselves to serve the world— making manifold injustices right, overcoming oppression, restoring the world to communion with God. Only God's grace can empower such service. Only God's love can nourish such a spirit. The challenge confronts us: to become God's agents to transform the world with divine love.

1. Scott, "The Authority of Love," in *Authority in the Anglican Communion,* ed. Stephen W. Sykes (Toronto: Anglican Book Center, 1987), p. 67.

Heterosexism: A Challenge to Ecumenical Solidarity

Virginia Ramey Mollenkott

I GREW up lesbian in the Plymouth Brethren Assemblies. Thus I have a firsthand acquaintance with heterosexism. Plymouth Brethren have been accurately described by Garrison Keillor: although they are usually kind, they assume that homosexuality so violates God's order of things that gay and lesbian people are beyond the pale of humanity. My cousin's college-aged daughter once stared at me as if I were a rare species behind bars in a zoo; she was unable to contain satiric giggles as I attempted to make her acquaintance. Many fundamentalist schools institutionalize such attitudes, dismissing students discovered to be gay or lesbian (sometimes mere weeks before graduation), and firing excellent tenured teachers. The cruelty of confessing Christians can be breathtaking.

With regard to such cruelty, I speak about *heterosexism* rather than *homophobia* for strategic reasons. It is too easy for

Virginia Ramey Mollenkott, an Episcopalian, is Professor of English at William Paterson College in Wayne, New Jersey. She is the author of ten books, including Godding: Human Responsibility and the Bible *and (with Letha Scanzoni)* Is the Homosexual My Neighbor?

people to interpret a phobia as a morbid personal matter. A phobia can be someone else's private abnormality. To speak about heterosexism, however, bears witness that the basic phenomenon is public, institutionalized prejudice against gay and lesbian people throughout this society.

I internalized this heterosexism and the accompanying self-hatred so thoroughly that I married at age twenty-one, although I knew myself to be lesbian at age twelve. Like everyone in my environment, I believed that heterosexual marriage (or heterosexual celibacy) was God's will for the entire human race. Wanting to please God and my family, and hoping that "normal feelings would follow normal behavior," I married myself into an oppression that lasted for more than seventeen years.

Heterosexism is akin to political "isms" that all of us share to some degree: racism, sexism, ageism, classism, militarism, and handicapism (including the classist/weightist assumption that "you can never be too rich or too thin"). These "isms" establish economic and political structures that are difficult to speak to because they are difficult to *see*. Such structures so pervade our society that they seem to be God's order of things. This results in great suffering for some persons, persons whose pain may be alleviated as they become aware that the structures are not God's but humanity's.

When "isms" remain unconscious, their power over our behavior is considerable. When my husband argued that his will was law by virtue of his being a man, I was defeated—not by the superior logic of his argument but because sexist assumptions (legitimated by the patriarchal God) had beclouded my brain. The power of such assumptions is so profound that as I became aware that my marriage had not "healed" my homosexuality, I endured the abuse, even knowing it was abuse. My husband often said that if I were a mature woman I would enjoy submitting to his will, since submission is the nature of woman. My own hidden heterosexism, which I had internalized from without, whispered, "Maybe he's right. How would you know? *You're not a normal woman.*"

It is not easy to confront the power of the "isms" and to redirect our patterns of thinking into more just and truthful paths. I began not with my heterosexism but with my white racism. After I spoke out in an article in *Christianity Today*, I received my first hate mail. Next I addressed sexism. Slowly, I came to see how entangled racism and sexism and classism are. Militarism, handicapism, ageism, and Christian triumphalism (including destructive dominion over the earth) were matters I subsequently studied.

But to address heterosexism I needed the assistance of many gay brothers and lesbian sisters. These sisters and brothers I found in the Universal Fellowship of Metropolitan Community Churches and at Kirkridge retreat center, among other places. Maya Angelou has said that it would be wise for all African-Americans to visit a free African nation to see how African peoples comport themselves when they are the normative group, and how they exercise their political power. While there is no nation for gay and lesbian people to visit, there is the Universal Fellowship of Metropolitan Community Churches, and there are other gay and lesbian Christian organizations and conferences. As I visited in these settings, I saw that gay and lesbian people are warm, responsible, and deeply spiritual, altogether unlike the fearsome caricatures planted in my mind by heterosexist socialization.

It still took me many years to stop feeling like I needed a shower whenever I spoke to someone about my lesbian identity. For a long time it was easier for me to advocate justice for gay and lesbian people than to identify myself as one of them. Along the way I was astonished as I became aware of how well I had been trained in male-identified heterosexism, and how ill-equipped I was to focus on myself. When asked about something as simple as my favorite color, I panicked. I had focused so completely on what my husband and others (especially men) wanted from me that I did not know my own color preference. I did not know my own heart's desires. As I made these discoveries I also had to address my childhood experience of incest, an experience that led me to distrust my own perceptions in a severe way and intensified the heterosexism I had internalized. In addition, I had to confront my fear in the face of the possibilities of not pleasing those I loved, of not having first-class citizenship, of not being able to practice my ministry through teaching. At last, at the core of my being, I sensed a go-ahead signal from the Spirit. I spoke openly about being lesbian and began to live in unqualified solidarity with God's lesbian daughters and gay sons. The empowerment and joys of this liberation are inexpressible and ineffable, like a mystical experience.

My hope is that ecumenists will enter into solidarity with gay and lesbian people. Ecumenists have long since challenged traditional denominationalism by pleading for partnership rather than triumphal separatism. Thus a foundation for further extensions of solidarity is present. Also present and deeply felt is the pain of many gay and lesbian persons who feel called to serve God in ordained ministry in various churches. Some relegate their sexuality to the private sphere, closeted in frequently fearful secrecy. Some, living in long-term covenantal relationship, endure being physically separated by many miles by the decree of church officials, knowing that to reveal their distress would also reveal their life partnership and end their ministry. Their screams may be silent in the churches, but I am sure that they resound in God's ears.

The heterosexist structures of church and society cause pain for many more persons than those gay and lesbian people who want to be ordained. Many women are trapped in battering marriages that the church blessed and blesses. Many children suffer abuse—physical, sexual, emotional—often in the name of upholding the family unit as envisioned by the church. And yet there is emerging evidence—biblical, theological, historical, medical—which makes it increasingly manifest that the hetero-sexist system is not ordained by God but is as iniquitous in God's eyes as racism and classism and militarism.[1]

The question I put to my ecumenical colleagues at this time is whether we care about solidarity with *all* God's oppressed people. Rhetoric will come closer to reality when some of the most silenced members of the so-called second sex, God's lesbian daughters, are recognized and welcomed home. We are everywhere, awaiting a response.

1. Among the resources making this emerging evidence available are these: John J. McNeill, *The Church and the Homosexual,* 3rd ed. (Boston: Beacon Press, 1988); Letha Scanzoni and Virginia Mollenkott, *Is the Homosexual My Neighbor? Another Christian View* (New York: Harper & Row, 1980); John Boswell, *Christianity, Social Tolerance, and Homosexuality: Gay People in Western Europe from the Beginning of the Christian Era to the Fourteenth Century* (Chicago: University of Chicago Press, 1981); Robin Scroggs, *The New Testament and Homosexuality* (Philadelphia: Fortress Press, 1984); and George R. Edwards, *Gay-Lesbian Liberation: A Biblical Perspective* (New York: Pilgrim Press, 1984). Boswell, for example, has discovered that, whereas the church did not declare heterosexual marriage to be a sacrament until 1215 C.E., one of the earliest Greek liturgical documents is a marriage ceremony for two persons of the same sex. The document dates to the fourth century, if not earlier. In other words, nine centuries before heterosexual marriage was declared a sacrament, the church liturgically celebrated same-sex covenants. The request of gay and lesbian people is that the contemporary church restore an ancient privilege.

Choose Life: Reflections of a Black African-American Roman Catholic Woman Religious Theologian

Jamie T. Phelps, O.P.

A S I look around me, I see many of my extended blood family of African-Americans suffering disproportionately from the ravages of economic poverty, hunger, poor housing, inadequate education, disease, high infant mortality, and low life-expectancy. The current condition of African-Americans is rooted in our history of oppression under slavery, segregation, and racism. The most devastating effects have been twofold: first, the internalization of negative views of our race and culture manifest in self-hatred and self-destruction, in turn evident in suicide, black-on-black murder, and drug abuse; second, African-Americans' separation from the rich, positive spiritual traditions of our own African and slave ancestors.

The screams of my black brothers and sisters who are economically poor call me and challenge my African-American middle-class privatized spiritual solitude. The screams of my

Jamie T. Phelps, O.P., is Assistant Professor of Doctrinal Theology and Chairperson of the Department of Doctrinal and Historical Studies at the Catholic Theological Union in Chicago, Illinois. She is a member of the Adrian Dominican Sisters.

black brothers and sisters who are economically poor propel me to speak out against the institutional racism and sexism that infect every aspect of life in our society and in our churches. The screams of my black brothers and sisters who are economically poor drive me to seek ways to construct or transform institutions so that my brothers' and sisters' cries for freedom and justice and for recognition of their human dignity, intelligence, and creativity will be heard. God hears the cries of my brothers and sisters. Do we?[1]

Although I experience oppression because of my race and gender, I have not internalized this oppression. My family taught me the truth about myself. My parents taught me to love my black skin ("the darker the berry, the sweeter the juice"), to treasure the poetry and music and dance of African-Americans, along with the "classics" and folk art of other peoples. My parents introduced me to the reality of God's love for me and began my appreciation of the history of my people's ability to hope in the midst of hopelessness because of our faith.

Although I experience marginalization and treatment as a non-person in many of my contacts with the dominant culture, my pain is only momentary because, by the grace of the Spirit, I have acquired a sense of self-esteem and self-knowledge that is not dependent on the affirmation of my oppressors. Years of study, prayer, and growth in faith under the influence of the Spirit have helped me shed the veils of colonization and slavery and drink deeply of the fresh waters of racial pride and self-affirmation. My pride and affirmation of "the soul of the black people" is rooted in the reality of the wisdom of God's creation—"And God saw everything that [God] had made, and . . . it was very good" (Gen. 1:31)—and the mystery of God's entrance into humanity through the Incarnation. So I live mentally with a post-colonized and post-slavery worldview of race

1. Cf. "Gaudium et Spes," 1, in *Vatican Council II: The Conciliar and Post-Conciliar Documents* (New York: Costello Publishers, 1980).

and culture, affirming my own race and culture while at the same time I am open to the goodness of each nation, race, gender, and human being, and of all God's creation. My daily struggle is not so much with the question of my own life as with the question of the lives of black families who are economically or spiritually poor, and the spiritual lives of members of the dominant culture who are insensitive, indifferent, or hostile to African-Americans as well as to other racially and culturally oppressed groups, especially women.

In my search for the meaning of my life in faith, I have discovered the biblical tradition that affirms the worth of African-American life (both male and female) and my internal impulse to seek the conditions of freedom that nurture, sustain, and enhance this life. The Hebrew scriptures speak of God placing before us the choice of life and death, urging us to choose life: "I have set before you life and death . . . ; therefore choose life, that you and your descendants may live" (Deut. 30:19). The New Testament clearly indicates that Jesus came to this earth to give us life: "I came that they may have life, and have it abundantly" (John 10:10).

The *central message* of Jesus' preaching was the coming of the kingdom or rule of God. The *central acts* of Jesus (preaching and miracles of healing) were acts that signaled the kingdom as the reality of God's rule breaking into human history. The early Christian communities recognized and remembered Jesus as one who called the poor, the oppressed, and the marginalized to himself and then sent them, in the freedom of their new identity, to proclaim the good news. The early Christian communities remembered Jesus as one who challenged those who acted as false gods either by civil-political domination or by religious tyranny. He called all to new life and to right relationships in a re-ordered and just society within the diverse cultures and peoples of his time.

These days only a few prophetic voices speak and act to challenge the conventions of racism, sexism, and cultural imperialism that infect our daily lives within our society and churches. Leaders in many churches, as well as in social and political spheres of life, have all too often accommodated the teachings of the gospel to social, economic, and political conventions of the day. Seduced by the wisdom of a world centered on technological advancement and business profitability rather than on the quality of life for all people, many Christians— black and white—fail to acknowledge the increased numbers of poor. Many Christians fail to see that these poor are victims of the prosperity we enjoy as the costs of medical care, housing, education, and technical training soar beyond the reach of the poor majority.[2] Many fail to see that more black men are incarcerated in jails than have access to higher education. Segregated social activity and housing have gone unchallenged and at times have been urged by Christians who have not taught that racism is sin because it divides human community.[3]

Life for black African-Americans within predominantly white Christian churches is characterized by the same general indifference and marginalization that marks and mars their life in the larger society. This segregation, along with the domination of women and racial-ethnic minorities in ecclesial affairs, including "de facto" exclusion from official ecclesial ministry and theological training, is accepted without challenge. Even those who enter seminaries, formation houses for religious orders, or graduate theological schools are confronted by the reality that the rich religious and cultural heritage of black African-Americans and of other racial-ethnic peoples who are oppressed has no place within the required curriculum.

Some Christian leaders, however, have seen the oppression

2. See William J. Wilson, *The Truly Disadvantaged: The Inner City, the Underclass and Public Policy* (Chicago: University of Chicago Press, 1987).

3. See *Brothers and Sisters to Us: U.S. Catholic Pastoral on Racism in Our Day* (Washington, D.C.: United States Catholic Conference, 1979). See also National Research Council, *A Common Destiny: Blacks and American Society* (Washington, D.C.: National Academy Press, 1989).

and have heard the challenge of the gospel. I have heard my brother bishops state that "social justice is an essential element of the gospel" and denounce the sin of racism within the Roman Catholic Church.[4] I have heard biblical interpretations which assure me that the religious, economic, social, and political oppression of black African-Americans, as well as of other racial-ethnic peoples who are oppressed, is not in accord with the rule of God and the gospel that Jesus preached.[5]

What I have not heard is the rustle of a movement of masses of white and black Christians in the predominantly white Christian churches to address *concretely* the oppressed conditions of black African-Americans. We have been anesthetized by a privatistic and spiritualized interpretation of the Bible and by ecclesial traditions indifferent to the social and spiritual condition of people of different cultures and races. There are few systematic attempts to combat racism or to work at an inculturation of the concerns of African-Americans within the structures and liturgies of churches. This indifference is deepened because few black African-Americans have decision-making power within these churches.

Black African-Americans within predominantly white Christian churches, both Catholic and Protestant, are often cut off from the rich mainstream of African-American religious traditions.[6] Yet the Spirit is undaunted by the institutional limits of church and society and finds response in the hearts of some

4. See *Brothers and Sisters to Us*. See also "Justice in the World," in *Renewing the Earth: Catholic Documents on Peace, Justice and Liberation*, ed. David J. O'Brien and Thomas A. Shannon (New York: Image Books, 1977).

5. See "Populorum Progressio," in *Renewing the Earth: Catholic Documents on Peace, Justice and Liberation*. See also *Economic Justice for All: Pastoral Letter on Catholic Social Teaching and the U.S. Economy* (Washington, D.C.: National Conference of Catholic Bishops, 1986).

6. See Gayraud S. Wilmore, *Black Religion and Black Radicalism* (Maryknoll, N.Y.: Orbis Books, 1973). See also *Black Theology: A Documentary History, 1966-1979*, ed. Gayraud S. Wilmore and James H. Cone (Maryknoll, N.Y.: Orbis Books, 1979).

black and white members and leaders of predominantly white churches.

Both white and black churches will stand in judgment before God. Predominantly white churches are called to decide whether they will embrace the prophetic tradition and become prophets to the nation or whether they will continue to ratify a social order that devalues and destroys black life and black families. Black churches are called to decide whether they will continue to be nurturing havens for black life against the assault of other institutions *as well as* continue the prophetic traditions of our African-American religious tradition that stood up against the social and ecclesial forces denying the life and spiritual riches of black African-Americans.

God created part of the worldwide human family black African-American and saw that it was very good. God places before the Christian churches—both Catholic and Protestant—the choice of life or death. We choose life if we live in accord with God's rule, using our spiritual and material resources to benefit the life of black African-Americans as well as other racially and ethnically oppressed cultures and women. We choose death if we "know what is right to do and fail to do it" (James 4:17). Choose life!

Outside the Gate: The Challenge of the Universal Fellowship

Janet E. Pierce

TODAY women challenge the church to grant women full participation in church leadership; women who are also lesbian challenge the church to openly invite them to any participation. Daily I deal with the damage done lesbians and gay men because the church has told them they cannot be part of God's domain. The church has taught and continues to teach that lesbians and gay men are not saved through Jesus Christ. The basic concern of my people during the Ecumenical Decade is not a position in the hierarchy; it is salvation.

I pastor a small congregation—about 150 members—of the Universal Fellowship of Metropolitan Community Churches in Huntsville, Alabama. The congregation is less than three years old, and members come from a variety of denominational backgrounds. Most of the members left the church of their childhood when they were adolescents. For many of them,

Janet E. Pierce is pastor of the Metropolitan Community Church in Huntsville, Alabama. She is a liaison to the NCC's Commission on Faith and Order, representing the Universal Fellowship of Metropolitan Community Churches.

involvement with the Metropolitan Community Church represents their first adult commitment to Christ.

The Universal Fellowship of Metropolitan Community
Churches was founded in 1968 by a former Pentecostal
preacher, Troy Perry. Reverend Perry felt called to found a
church in which all God's people would be welcomed. The
initial vision for the Universal Fellowship was that the gospel
be preached to gay men and lesbians, persons who had been
told that the gospel was not for them. The Universal Fellowship
of Community Churches is a Christian, post-denominational
church whose simple doctrine encourages diversity in theology
and in Christian living. Consequently, the Universal Fellowship
has the potential to draw from the vast riches of Christian
traditions.

Sunday mornings at local Metropolitan Community
Churches reflect this richness. Services include diverse elements of worship drawn from a variety of traditions, and the
call to the communion table is an open invitation. As the people
come to the table, some bow, some cross themselves, some
genuflect; one man weeps as he receives communion for the
first time in twenty years. The people come to the table singly,
in pairs, and in small groups to receive God's gift and to pray,
each of them experiencing in communion, in his or her own
way, the tangible presence of God. As communion continues,
the congregation joins in song, at some services rising spon-
taneously to express the joy of a shared experience of unity.
Jennie Boyd-Bull reflects on the source of this joy:

> Excommunication (outside the gate of the feast) has been used
> for centuries by the Christian church to discipline "sinners." As
> gays and lesbians, our experience of being "outside the gate,"
> often literally excommunicated from other churches, gives us the
> unique and wondrous joy of knowing that Christ's presence is
> beyond all "marriage," all legal boundaries for "communicating"
> in relationship. Matthew 9:10-13 [the story of Jesus eating with
> tax collectors and sinners] speaks this truth. . . . We know that

in the resurrection Jesus comes especially to free the oppressed, to reach the Samaritan woman (John 4), the Ethiopian eunuch (Acts 8), the "sexual sinner outside the gate" of every age, who is not judged by culture's rules, not even those of the institutional church, but by the love of God that is broader than human minds.[1]

Caught up in the demands of the daily struggle, the Universal Fellowship of Metropolitan Community Churches too often forgets the radical statement its very existence makes. It is a church in which gay men and lesbians who have been told they cannot be Christian experience the love of Christ. It is a church in which a Southern Baptist sits in communion with a Roman Catholic. It is a church in which theology happens more often than it is talked about. Indeed, the Universal Fellowship of Metropolitan Community Churches embodies much of what is hoped for in the ecumenical movement. We are a church of outcasts challenged to be the church of Jesus Christ.

Although we are a church made up of both women and men, our liberation within the Body of Christ is integrally related to the role and progress of women in the church. The same patriarchal system whose power is used to limit opportunities for women's ministry is likewise used to condemn and exclude lesbians and gay men. Sherri Boothman makes this point forcefully:

> Patriarchy is the source of the Christian churches' oppression of women and of gay/lesbian people. Gay men are considered bad because they are acting like women. This, of course, is a view based on ignorance. Gay men are men who have sex with other men; they are not acting like women. Even if one wants to claim, however, that they are acting like women, what is wrong with acting like a woman? In Augustine's eyes, it was wrong for a man

---

1. Boyd-Bull, "The Eucharist as Embodiment: Toward a Sacramental Theology," unpublished paper, Universal Fellowship of Metropolitan Community Churches, 1983, pp. 12-13.

to act like a woman because he was lowering himself to a second-class spiritual status, thus moving away from God, thus sin-
ning. If it is as good to be a woman as it is to be a man, then the
basis of the condemnation of homosexuality disappears in Christian theology. Christian churches will have to continue their
oppression of women in order to maintain our condemnation [the
condemnation of gay men and lesbians]; and they will have to
recognize the full equality and mutuality of women as human
creatures in order for us to know our liberation from their condemnation. This means massive changes in traditional Christian
theology, worship, and church administrative systems if we are
going to heal this ancient communal brokenness.[2]

In many ways it is good to be a woman in ministry in the
Universal Fellowship of Metropolitan Community Churches.
There is balanced male/female participation at all levels of
leadership: over 40 percent of all clergy are women, and women
are equally represented in all areas of oversight. In addition, the
Universal Fellowship is committed to an inclusivity that goes
beyond inclusive language to address issues of accessibility for
all people. Accordingly, we have done more than address issues
of language; we have also addressed issues as diverse as white
individuals working to heal racism and the removal of barriers
that physically limit participation in worship by individuals who
are differently abled.

Nevertheless, patriarchy is pervasive. Even with the participation of women at all levels of church leadership, patriarchal
thinking and patterns of behavior are powerful and pervasive
in the Universal Fellowship. As the denomination grows, we
continue to make efforts to ensure that its leadership remains
responsive to the needs and desires of its grassroots members.
Although a number of structural changes have been made to
try to ensure this responsiveness, various individual and cor-

2. Boothman, *Sexual Sin/Sexual Healing* (Los Angeles: Universal Fellowship Press, 1988), p. 5.

porate instances of hoarding power have meant that the structure hasn't always functioned in the way it was intended to. Since we all were formed by patriarchal structures, it is not easy to envision and enact alternatives.

At a local level, the goals of fully understanding and implementing inclusivity are hampered by the sexism, racism, able-bodyism, and classism that each of us has learned from society and from the churches in which we were raised. Although the Universal Fellowship has committed itself as a denomination to issues of inclusivity, local churches vary in their consistency and level of commitment. In addition, horizontal violence—which occurs when oppressed people lack recourse against their oppressors and so vent their anger and frustration on each other—is a problem for most oppressed people, and the lesbian and gay community is no exception.

Denominationally, as the Universal Fellowship has gained experience with women's participation at all levels of leadership, more subtle forms of sexism have surfaced. Issues that have recently come to the fore include equity in pay, women's involvement in pastoring larger congregations, and women becoming scapegoats at denominational levels of leadership. A recently re-formed women's commission is struggling with these and other women's issues. Some want to strengthen the denomination's commitment to combatting sexism. Others believe that the Universal Fellowship has already gone too far in its efforts at inclusivity.

Despite the difficulties of creating a church where leadership is shared at all levels with all people, the Universal Fellowship of Metropolitan Community Churches has made significant strides, and it continues to be one of the best places to be a woman in ministry. Indeed, the church's very foundation is the firm conviction that the systemic exclusion of anyone from the Body of Christ is a great sin. From my particular context, the challenge of lesbians to the church of Jesus Christ is a biblical one: "Go therefore and teach all nations, baptizing them in the name of the Creator and of Christ and of the Holy Ghost" (Matt. 28:19). For too long the church has refused its mandate to preach the good news to all God's people, including lesbians and gay men.

A Southern Baptist Pastor Speaks

Nancy Sehested

IT was a week of internal tug-of-war. I was speaking at a national conference on Christian-Jewish dialogue, a conference being boycotted by the Home Mission Board of the Southern Baptist Convention. In this controversial context, I spoke with some leaders of the Home Mission Board, including the president. The subject was women as pastors. I was offering my now-familiar lines: "Yes, God can and does call women to be pastors. There is evidence all around us. Just look and see." I was receiving their usual responses: "Women can serve, but it isn't biblical for women to be pastors." A back-and-forth volley ensued: "Yes, we can be pastors." "No, you can't." "Yes, we can." "No, you can't." This external exchange translated into my internal tug-of-war. There seemed to be no resolution on either front.

My internal tug-of-war was further intensified this week as I responded to several crisis situations involving individuals and families in my congregation as well as to my daughter, who

---

Nancy Sehested is pastor of the Prescott Memorial Baptist Church in Memphis, Tennessee.

became critically ill. In addition, there was the usual round of weekly demands: the newsletter, the Wednesday night service, the planning of Sunday worship, sermon preparation, meetings, visits, phone calls, and so on. Even as my lips were enunciating "Yes, we can," my own life experience made me wonder whether the leaders of the Home Mission Board were right—"No, you can't."

When my life had calmed down a bit, I recognized the question that churches really need to address today: "Can *anyone* be a pastor?" Many more questions follow that one. What do churches want, need, and expect from pastors? Do churches want a good preacher? teacher? counselor? Do churches want a good administrator and program planner? Do churches want a good recruiter and personnel manager? a crisis mediator? a spiritual companion and guide? The message from churches is mixed. On the one hand, most churches are mature enough to know that no one person can do all these things. On the other hand, conversations still suggest that churches are clinging to impossible expectations of the person who fills the position of pastor. Bloodshot congregational eyes continue to search the horizon for *someone* to come along *someday* and do it *all*.

A variety of solutions have been suggested for the problem of clergy over-extension: time management, stress management, personal therapy, guilt reduction exercise. My idea is to start "Churchaholics Anonymous," where people like me could make an important declaration: "Hello. My name is Nancy. I am a churchaholic. I am powerless to overcome this thing called church." This is a more honest admission that I am weak in the face of the institutional power of the church. This is an admission that clergy over-extension and burnout are psychological terms for spiritual death. Churches and pastors together must confront this terminal disease we have caught from our culture: the disease named *MORE*, manifest as the compulsive need for order, control, maintenance, and management, which makes our spiritual selves shrivel.

Our disease is deepened by the ancient affirmation that pastors are to be "without blemish." This has roots in the Hebrew law and prophets. The Hebrew word for "blemish" denotes anything that is abnormal or deviates from the set standard, whether physical, moral, or ritualistic in nature. Hebrew law required that animals offered for sacrifice be without blemish, and the law extended that requirement to include the one offering the sacrifice. Leviticus 21:17-23 makes this clear: "None of your descendants, from generation to generation, who has a defect, may draw near to offer the bread of his God. . . . He may not come near the veil or approach the altar, because he has a blemish, that he may not profane [the Lord's] sanctuaries." Churches and pastors have held to this tradition. Consequently, we have had too many pastors who thought they *could* be perfect. And we have had too few pastors with physical handicaps, since in Leviticus perfection of the body becomes symbolic of perfection of the soul.

As a woman pastor I wrestle with particular pressures today. The historical moment has placed women pastors in a spotlight that can be blinding. We and our work are under magnifying-glass scrutiny. And when I speak, I am still resisting the centuries-old gravity that works to pull women back into their seats and to keep them silent and smiling. When I speak, I also sense solidarity with an invisible cloud of women witnesses who are standing with me and begging me to break the sound barrier for them too. It is a wonder—one of God's wonders—that any of us attempt to be pastors at all.

One of my temptations is to be a model, and I am tempted to push my church to be a model as well. I want us to be models so we can show the world that it can be done, so we can say, "See, women can pastor—successfully!" But neither I nor the church is called to be a model for anyone else. We are called to be faithful to God's unique call to us. A by-product of our faithfulness might be that other people on the path look to us and are encouraged. But this is God's business, not ours.

As a woman paid to be a pastor, I also wrestle with my Baptist heritage of "the priesthood of all believers" (perhaps today we should say "the pastorhood of all believers"). How do Baptist churches embody this heritage today? Is there one capital "P" for *the* Pastor, with everyone else stuck in the lower-case "p"? Could a recovery of this heritage be a resource in response to clergy over-extension and burn-out? As I address these questions, I am confronted by questions about authority and power and questions about the nature of Christian leadership as well.

As I wrestle, my hope is not in women's superior ability to resist the temptations of our institutions. Women are as susceptible as men to the seductive dangers deeply embedded in institutional life. None of us is immune to the enticement of praise for workaholic patterns. Like men, women can succumb to a system that sucks the spirit and the life right out of us. Religious institutions can knock us women along with the men into a state of amnesia about God's reign.

My hope comes from this moment in history. In this moment I hear God saying, "I have new wine and you are called to put it in new wineskins. The old wineskins will burst if you try to hold new wine in them. If you just replace a man with a woman, not only will the old skins burst; the new wine will be ruined. Put new wine in new wineskins, so there will be life anew for all." My hope comes from God, who is building a new household on land leveled as mountains have been laid low and valleys raised up, so all may stand on the same holy ground. My hope will be fulfilled as we choose to participate in God's leveling and rebuilding. I see walls coming down between clergy and laity. I see handicapped people entering the household. I see a homecoming for people who have been alienated or excluded. I see people singing Bach chorales and gospel tunes, tapping their feet together. I see rich and poor living together in the household where no one will hunger. I see children laughing, women dancing, men crying for joy, then women laughing, children crying for joy, men dancing, and all mingling together.

I see a people who heeds God's choosing "what is foolish in the world to shame the wise, . . . what is weak in the world to shame the strong, . . . what is low and despised in the world, even things that are not, to bring to nothing things that are" (1 Cor. 1:27-28). I see it.

I am called to keep alive this vision of who we are called to be. I am called to be a rabbi in the community, telling God's story and our story and setting them in conversation with each other. I am called to be one among the people to empower each one to exercise God's call in his or her life. I am called to be as fully human as I can be to call forth our full humanity as a corporate body.

But I still struggle to see the path for pastors. The structures that could embody this call are not clear to me. For now, the image of a journey illumines the way ahead. There are several things I bring along with me on this journey into the unknown. I bring my longing to know God. I bring my suffering, which keeps me within arm's reach of others who suffer. I bring my joy in celebrating lives created in the image of God. I bring my hope grounded in God, for whom nothing is beyond redemption, not even clericalism and church institutionalism, and with whom I see a vision of the new creation. My hope is a matter of spiritual discipline. I create hope as I walk on with the sure step of one who has heard her name called. I pray that with each step my love for God, neighbor, and myself may increase.

A Lutheran Woman Looks at the Decades

Amalie R. Shannon

WHEN a woman has passed the significant benchmark of the scriptural "three score years and ten," perhaps it is understandable that she should have a sense of déjà vu when asked to write of "challenges, solidarity, alienation, and wrestling" in relation to women's experience in the institutional church. Moreover, the request that these thoughts emphasize personal perspectives creates a certain discomfort for a woman of my heritage and generation. A further reservation is the knowledge that we who make up the church must resist the temptation to succumb to solipsistic thinking, to concentrate on our separate identities as women, men, clergy, laity, or national and racial constituencies. Our focus should be on our oneness in Christ, because the aspirations and concerns of women are as diverse as those of any group classified by one of

---

Amalie R. Shannon is a retired college vice-president who has represented her church as a delegate to assemblies of the World Council of Churches and the Lutheran World Federation. She has also served on the National Lutheran Council, the Lutheran Council, USA, and the Commission for a New Lutheran Church.

their common characteristics—in this case, gender. Like men, women exemplify the whole spectrum of convictions, capabilities, strengths, and weaknesses.

In the earlier decades of my life, I—as a daughter, sister, niece, and cousin of ordained Lutheran ministers—grew up with the highest respect for the office of the ministry and those called to it. In childhood and adolescence I accepted without question my exclusion from that high calling because of my gender. Not until long after I became a minister's wife and mother of three children did I begin to be puzzled by the fact that male pronouncements were widely accepted simply because they were *ipso facto* male. Since my own gifts tended toward analysis and inquiry, I soon observed that such female contributions were not highly valued, even in informal theological discussion. I had not been "called"; I had no "authority." It seemed I could not expect to join in serious exchange with equal status. More bemused than angered, I earned a doctorate and pursued a satisfying career in higher education.

During the 1960s, Lutheran theologian Philip J. Hefner pointed out that the role of women in the Lutheran Church was that church's greatest "hidden" problem. This explicit acknowledgment reinforced my own perceptions. Thus I was elated when, in 1970, the efforts of committed lay women and others culminated in a vote by the Lutheran Church in America to ordain women to the office of the ministry, giving them official recognition as equal to their male counterparts. Yet twenty years later, ordained women continue to encounter obstacles to their vocational fulfillment and careers.

Three of my experiences exemplify the perpetuation of the denial of the institutional church's full acceptance of women.

In the late 1970s, a leading international churchman eloquently pleaded for greater understanding of the needs of the poor in economically underdeveloped countries. He stressed not only the need for physical assistance but also the yearning for self-esteem and acceptance. As a member of a panel interviewing him and assessing his presentation, I noted that he had made no reference to women and their unique need for full acceptance. His reply—that he had little time or sympathy for the concerns of middle-class American women—evoked audible gasps from many in the audience. The church surely cannot expect its women to accept such demeaning treatment of their dignity and talents.

The struggle again emerged in 1982 when seventy Lutherans were elected to serve as a commission for a new Lutheran Church (leading to what is presently called the Evangelical Lutheran Church in America). This commission was chosen through a complicated process to ensure equal representation of laity, clergy, women, men, and diverse ethnic constituencies. If the results were not ideal, they did give strong witness to the universality of Christ's ministry and to the cherished Lutheran concept of "the priesthood of all believers." For the duration of its existence, the commission endured the caustic critiques of those who viewed it as a group that was incompetent and "knew nothing about the church," as one critic put it. These critics were dismayed that persons other than white male theologians were making decisions about the new church.

At an early session of this commission, there was a long, heated discussion about equal representation on its committees and task forces. The strength of conviction and strong emotion surrounding this issue bewildered many on the commission. Some decried the amount of time "wasted" on this topic and only reluctantly accepted the majority vote adopting equal representation as a working principle.

For decades I had been loathe to see specific percentages adopted to mandate diverse representation. But when my life-time experience was reinforced by my experience on the commission, I acceded to what I perceived to be the necessity of such a mandate. Resistance persisted. At one point a bishop tried to evade the principle in committee appointments, and it was necessary to vote once again to reaffirm the principle in the face of opposition by three top clergymen.

Ultimately the principle of diverse representation was incorporated into the documents of the newly formed Evangelical Lutheran Church in America. There were those who had argued that our Christian commitment and sense of fair play would naturally bring about equity, but the elections and major appointments in the new ELCA were disillusioning. Among the 65 new bishops appointed, there were no women; among those elected to head the staffs of major divisions, there was only one woman—chosen, predictably, to head the staff of the women's commission. Tokenism persists. If current rumblings against what has unfortunately been dubbed the "quota system" result in revision of ELCA documents, it is clear that some intentional language must be used to sustain even a minimal adherence to representative equity in a church that aspires to be inclusive.

In 1984, the Lutheran World Federation assembled in Budapest, Hungary, for more than two weeks. Days passed with the dais dominated by the male officers and staff; one female, a secretary, sat alone to the side at the rear. Ultimately we women attending the assembly, cognizant of the action of previous assemblies and of official pronouncements affirming the role of women, staged a dignified protest. Women from all the nations represented participated in large numbers, and two expressed their pained concern over the federation's continuing discrimination. As a result, women presided over two sessions, but soon even that concession was withdrawn. Later, however, action was taken at a business plenary to assure greater representation of women in the leadership of the Lutheran World Federation. At the 1990 assembly of the federation in Curitiba, Brazil, more women had significant roles, although privately several women expressed anger that so few women were among the chief leaders of the closing six-hour festival.

I confess to a sense of bafflement, sorrow, and shame that the Christian church, the institution which has been a primary influence in forming the values of most of its members, has not been in the vanguard of affirming women as full partners in humanity. Yet we Lutheran women find hope in the decade ahead. Today women live in times recognizably different from the stagnant eighties, the evolving seventies, the turbulent sixties, and even earlier decades. Since I was born, women have won the right to vote, have gained control of their biology, and can now anticipate a significantly increased life expectancy. Nevertheless, political, sociological, economic, and moral resistance to equality is still pervasive.

The plans for the Ecumenical Decade lift our spirits and raise our hopes that the church may bring about a more substantial change in attitudes and actions, more openness to partnership of men and women in the church. The ELCA's new structure includes a commission for women that advocates such a partnership to make progress toward participation, justice, and spirituality in all the constituencies of institutional life. For one who has been impatient with serving as a "token" woman on Lutheran councils and committees in the sixties and seventies, the outlook is encouraging. We seek ecclesial and theological support for our struggle, support that liberates women for full ministry in and through the church. Weary of expending our energies on efforts to be recognized, we covet a theology that embraces all humanity on the same level of grace. Our vision for women emerging into new roles in our church is one in which God's will is that we, women and men, are one in Christ Jesus.

From One Orthodox Woman's Perspective

Stefanie Yova Yazge

WHAT exactly is ministry? What is ministry for women in the 1990s during the Ecumenical Decade of Churches in Solidarity with Women? I seek to translate my situation, which is not unique, into a challenge to the church during this decade.

Let me begin by defining my ministry. I am an Orthodox Christian woman with a master's degree in theological studies whose ministry is wide yet tends to be focused on liturgical theology and music. Presently (and probably for some time to come), I am using my training primarily in a parish setting. I am not restricted by clerical limitations or by bureaucratic structures in the church. I am in a potentially advantageous position, being a Christian woman with a better-than-average education who can work out my ministry in the great vineyard of Christ.

But since I am also a woman who was born and raised in one diocese and now has married into another, I do not have an "official" position or status. This means that I have no

Stefanie Yova Yazge ministers in the Antiochian Orthodox Church in Terre Haute, Indiana. She received her master's degree in theological studies from St. Vladimir's Seminary in Crestwood, New York.

"automatic" or assigned authority in the structures of the church. This in turn means that I have to find places where my talents may be best used and work to be heard when I believe my background is needed. Thus I am wrestling with what my ministry is and how I live it out and with what authority.

Many Orthodox women who are seminary-educated face the same situation that I do. The messages we receive are mixed. Many of my contemporary male counterparts, mostly clergy, have accepted me. My seminary professors have encouraged me. But the Orthodox Church is a hierarchical church with male-only clergy. There are those within that structure who do not look kindly on a woman who wants to be *too* involved, especially if she wants to be involved in liturgical theology. To be involved in liturgical theology is to step into a province that has usually been reserved for priests and bishops and has excluded both lay women and men. It is to ask questions about what liturgy is and what it means, about the reality it manifests in the order of services. When a woman questions or dares to urge the modification (or correction) of liturgical practice, some priests and bishops have been known to rather righteously imply or reply that a woman should mind her own business.

I contend that this response is rooted not in theology but in the cultural context out of which these priests and bishops come. Why? Because they have no theological leg upon which to stand to justify this response. The Orthodox Church teaches that everyone in authority exercises it *in* the church, not *over* the church. Accordingly, in addressing questions about or problems with or amendments to present practice, all members are responsible for participating for the sake of the community's future life and growth. In 1849 the Eastern Patriarchs (the bishops of the cities of Constantinople, Alexandria, Antioch, and Jerusalem) issued an encyclical which made this statement: "Neither Patriarchs nor Councils could then have introduced novelties amongst us, *because the protector of religion is the very body of the Church, even the people themselves.*" It is ironic that this statement is in a section of the encyclical concerning liturgical innovation deemed unacceptable by the patriarchs! But it is nonetheless clear that although the bishop is the one who is to "rightly divide the word" of God's truth, decisions are not to preclude the participation of the whole people of God.

This translates into a challenge to my church during the Ecumenical Decade. I do not necessarily propose that women be given official, paid positions in parishes or dioceses or archdioceses. The reality is that the Orthodox Church does not have many paid positions for men or women other than clerical positions. I do propose that people in positions of authority allow theologically educated women to participate whenever, wherever, and however we can in the life of the church. I challenge the church to encourage women and non-clerical men to become better-educated theologically and to receive the participation of these individuals without a patronizing or egotistical or turf-defending response. It is a challenge to all Christians to become better Christians, more Christ-like, for the sake of serving Christ, his church, and the world.

Some women may wonder why I do not challenge the church to include women among the ordained clergy, thereby providing women with an official position for ministry. Historically, the Orthodox Church has had the office of deaconess; currently there is discussion about reviving this office. But the ordination of women to the priesthood is not a matter for discussion, and we Orthodox women do not believe that the Orthodox Church is incorrect in its understanding of ordained priesthood as a male role or function. That this teaching may need contemporary explication does not negate its validity. As a woman, I do not feel that this teaching threatens or demeans or denies my own ministry.

This matter of ordained ministry takes me back to the 1988 meeting at Stony Point, New York, to initiate U.S. involvement in the Ecumenical Decade. I and the other Orthodox women there expressed our concern that this not be ten years dedicated to power politics and soapboxing for the ordination of women. We also articulated a problem we had with the phrase "Churches in Solidarity with Women." Does this mean that women exist as a separate group outside the church and that we are asking to be let in? And we also expressed puzzlement over the word "empowerment," used time and time again at the meeting. Empowered by whom, for what? Empowered for fighting our way into the church of which we supposedly do not feel we are a part? And the word "solidarity" brings to mind the struggle in Poland, a struggle that is essentially political. Is the Ecumenical Decade a call for political struggle within the church?

I contend that the church is not called to be in "solidarity" with anyone. Christ has given his church and invites us to be members of his body. We are called to be in solidarity with the church. The human element of the church is to be united with the divine nature as we overcome our fallenness and become what Christ truly created us to be. This understanding of the church raises questions that need to be addressed by both women *and men* in the church.

Perhaps what I am wrestling with as a woman during the Ecumenical Decade is how to engage non-Orthodox women in conversation about women's participation in the life of a church that does not ordain women. Too often Orthodox women are in ecumenical settings in which it is assumed that Orthodox women agree with more liberal, non-Orthodox hopes that the Orthodox Church will come to its contemporary senses, see beyond the ignorance of archaic patriarchal assumptions, and allow women to take their rightful place in the church's ministry. Too often we Orthodox women are the object of our ecumenical partners' pity. This attitude, which does not recognize and respect the experience and perspective of Orthodox women, must be addressed during the Ecumenical Decade if the decade is to be in solidarity with Orthodox women.

In all frankness, given the Ecumenical Decade's apparent

predisposition to feminist perspectives and given my church's limited financial resources, I fear that the participation of Orthodox women will be minimal. My greatest concern is that participation will be not only minimal but also without great commitment, lacking support from the hierarchy of the church and from Orthodox women themselves, who may well feel no ownership in such a decade because its underlying tone is foreign to their very being as Orthodox women.

Nevertheless, the Ecumenical Decade does genuinely challenge the Orthodox Church. It challenges my church to set aside barriers that are believed to be theological but that are actually non-theological. And it challenges my church to acknowledge and appreciate the ministries of women in the church, past and present. An acknowledgment and appreciation of these ministries is also the avenue through which Orthodox women may enter into dialogue with the decade.

Presents and Presence

Rena M. Yocom

ONE Christmas two elderly sisters received a silk flower arrangement from an estranged sister. They examined the gift and decided they did not want it. The arrangement did not match anything in their house. Besides, they judged that such an expensive gift was inappropriate given their sister's small pension. And so they "ungifted" the gift, sending it back to their sister.

Women have time and time again had the painful experience of the church "ungifting" our gifts. Our gifts are often deemed undesirable because they do not match the ecclesial furniture or because they are not like anything anybody has envisioned. Indeed, our very presence is not valued, just as the presents we bring are marked "return to sender." This "ungifting" is denial, denial of the giver as well as the gifts.

In these times, women are beginning to celebrate gifts, even

Rena M. Yocom is a diaconal minister in the United Methodist Church who is currently serving as Minister of Adult Education at Village Presbyterian Church in Prairie Village, Kansas. She is a member of the NCC's Faith and Order Commission and of its Executive Committee.

when and where "ungifting" is intended. Here is one testament to such celebrations of gifts. The pastor of a small congregation died. When the congregation could not find a new pastor, the pastor's widow answered the call. She attended seminary, integrating her learning into her ministry. One day the services of a plumber were needed at the parsonage. When the plumber arrived, he asked the woman whether her husband were the preacher. "No," she said, "I am." The plumber was dismayed: "Don't you know that Paul told women to be silent in church?" Lovingly, the pastor replied, "Bless you, child. Paul didn't call me. God did!" This woman is Leontine Kelley, a bishop in the United Methodist Church.

Methodists have been studying ministry since before they were *United* Methodists. Indeed, the ministerial differences between the Methodist Protestant Church and the Methodist Episcopal Churches have never been fully resolved. A number of factors—the merger with the Evangelical United Brethren, the fact that more and more women are in ministry, the timeliness of the diaconate, the expanding emphasis on lay ministry, and the increasing numbers who find that itineracy does not meet their needs—have added urgency and passion to our consideration of matters of ministry.

Significantly, a woman, Ruth Daugherty, has served as the chair of the current General Commission to Study Ministry. What began as a request for a theological statement became a springboard for discussion of the prerogatives and powers of particular offices in the church. Daugherty oversaw this conversion of the commission's task, recognizing that the commission's report could make an important contribution to continuing conversation about ministry. And she realized that the challenge of this continuing conversation was recognition that ministry begins with baptism. As a woman whose gifts had sometimes been "ungifted" by the church, she understood the significance of this recognition. She saw that for the church not to recognize the gifts of women for ministry is for the church not to recognize the validity of its own baptism of women.

Another challenge confronting the church during the Ecumenical Decade is that of inclusive language. Our language reveals our real intentions, regardless of our representative quotas and rhetoric. In all our language we are called to be intentionally inclusive. We who are United Methodists find our intentionality to be inclusive particularly challenged when we sing together. United Methodists have always sung their theology. This mark was imprinted by John and Charles Wesley, who formulated their foundational theology in the hymns they wrote. Accordingly, changing a hymn or creating a new hymnal is a matter of great significance for United Methodists.

Recently the United Methodist Church did receive a new hymnal. In the process of its creation, a woman on the Hymnal Revision Committee placed a red dot on every page of the old hymnal where gender limits were evident. The results were revealing, raising many questions for Reverend Beryl Ingram-Ward, pastor of St. Paul's United Methodist Church in Tacoma, Washington, and chair of the Ritual Committee of the Hymnal Revision Committee. How many "him hymns" are legitimate? How many "kings" and how many "fathers" can we sing about before we circumscribe our understanding of the very nature of God? May any "mother" hymns to God be included along with "father" hymns to God? How can a new hymnal do all it is expected to do—at once incorporate favorite hymns from the past, more gender-inclusive hymns, and hymns diverse enough to endure for decades—and still have theological integrity? These questions resounded for many women in the United Methodist Church.

As I think about the presents and presence of women in the church, I remember a special occasion when women's presence, presents, and the bonding of sisters were palpable to me. The season in the church's year was Pentecost. To the women who gathered in the Baptist Prayer House in Moscow, I was

"Deacon" Yocom, a Christian from the United States who had come to be with them, Christians in the USSR, so that we could pray together as the leaders of our nations met for a fourth Summit meeting. I had just offered the evening message. The air was electric with expectation. We spoke together about the leading of the Holy Spirit. We spoke together about the time for prayer and the time for peace. We were sisters in the faith. On this occasion I experienced the first Pentecost. I came to know how kindred spirits filled with God's Spirit could understand each other even through language barriers. On this evening, tears cleansed our hearts, and touches of our hands spoke eloquently.

Because of this occasion, I am also aware that one of the challenges during the Ecumenical Decade is a challenge to women to affirm the gifts of other women. We have long acknowledged that men are different from each other. But for too long we have not acknowledged our own differences and appreciated the different ministries to which we are called. It is painful when a woman who is an elder speaks pejoratively about another woman who chooses to be a diaconal minister (a permanent deacon), implying that a diaconal minister is only partly professional. It is painful when a woman who is a diaconal minister speaks pejoratively about a woman who chooses to be a lay woman, implying that she is not privy to the mysteries of the church and its ministry.

God is calling women and endowing them with a great diversity of gifts. Are we ready to receive God's gifts and one another? Is the church ready to receive our presents and our presence, honoring our baptism in the name of Jesus Christ, in whom there is neither male nor female?

II WOMEN AND THE ECUMENICAL MOVEMENT

Toward a Renewed Community of Women and Men

Joan Brown Campbell

ALTHOUGH the day was crisp and cold, the sun was shining as I boarded the Pan Am shuttle to Boston. I was on my way to join eight thousand other witnesses to the historic ordination of Barbara Clementine Harris as the first woman bishop in the Anglican Communion. I felt both anticipation and sadness as I boarded the shuttle. I anticipated the consecration, the first ordination of a woman bishop in the 450 years of Anglican tradition and an altogether unprecedented event in the two-thousand-year history of the church catholic. But I was also sad because I sensed that this victory was not won without pain, anger, rancor, and bitterness, and that the struggle was not over. The Boston setting bespoke the truth of my sense of sadness. As Harvey Cox put it when commenting on the ordination,

> Boston has never been particularly friendly to women preach-
> ers. . . . Within a decade of its founding the Puritan divines drove

---

Joan Brown Campbell, an ordained minister in the Christian Church (Disciples of Christ), is the Executive Director of the U.S. Office of the World Council of Churches in New York City.

Anne Hutchinson out of the colony for organizing a religious discussion group in her parlor—"not a fitting activity for women," they decreed. Then a few decades later the same serious gentlemen publicly hanged Mary Dyer, a Quaker, on the Common. The alleged witches of nearby Salem fared no less badly. So for a city where history always weighs heavy on the present, the consecration of Barbara Clementine Harris as Suffragen Bishop in the nation's largest Episcopal diocese did not go unnoticed either by the living or the dead.[1]

There is no doubt that there are those who will leave the Episcopal Church because of this historic event. But in Boston on the day of Barbara Harris's ordination, their voices were muted.

On this day, the Episcopal Church in the United States witnessed to the watching world that it is a church in solidarity with women. As fifty-five male bishops laid hands on this diminutive African-American woman, the Episcopal Church proclaimed that the power of God transmitted through the centuries was conferred upon Barbara Harris. Her ordination calls into question the assumption that only men can stand in the line of apostolic succession. This was indeed a quintessential witness to the church in solidarity with women.

As the hour-long parade of dignitaries processed into Hines Auditorium for the ordination, we passed by a young male Episcopal priest who cradled a newborn baby in his arms. When I greeted him, he said, "This is my daughter. I want her to remember this day." This young father understood that, for good or ill, the church would be different from this day forth. The all-male hierarchy would have to wrestle with an African-American woman in their midst. In the words of Reverend Paul Washington, preacher at the ordination, "You didn't just come here to see a woman being consecrated. You have come to see

1. Harvey Cox, "Big Day in Back Bay," *Christianity and Crisis*, 20 Mar. 1989, p. 78.

God, who with God's mighty hand has lifted up one who was at the bottom of society and has exalted her to sit in the chair to be one of God's chief pastors. The word of God is once again being made flesh in our midst."

Voices from other communions in the ecumenical movement expressed concern about the ordination. His Holiness Pope Shenouda, head of the Coptic Orthodox Church, said that the issue of the ordination of women was not a relevant issue for the Orthodox Church. But, he continued, "the consecration of Barbara Harris has put the issue of the ordination of women to the priesthood on our agenda again. We cannot ignore what is taking place in the Anglican communion." Pope John Paul II made it clear that he sees the ordination of Barbara Harris as an obstacle to unity. This view was also voiced by Reverend James Hopkinson Cupid, Jr., an Episcopal priest of the Diocese of New York. During the ordination ceremony, he stood to make a formal objection to Barbara Harris's ordination. He implored the presiding bishop not to proceed, saying that he believed "her consecration and election were contrary to sound doctrine and the consecration an intractable impediment to the realization of that visible unity of the church for which Christ prayed."

Although I disagree with the content of this concern for the unity of the church, I agree that this ordination will challenge our understanding of church unity. From my perspective, the unity of the church is inseparably bound together with the renewal of broken human community. These two fundamental ecumenical themes are stated in the study entitled "The Unity of the Church and the Renewal of Human Community" done by the Commission on Faith and Order of the World Council of Churches. This study makes clear that concern for the visible unity of Christ's church may never be considered apart from concern for Christian proclamation, witness, and service in a world crying out for renewal. To separate these two ecumenical tasks is to forget that Jesus' prayer for the unity of the church was for the sake of the world.

Upbuilding a renewed community of women and men is the particular task of God's people in our time. Christians all around the world are yearning for a more authentic community. This yearning for community has given rise to the Ecumenical Decade of the Churches in Solidarity with Women. If we were to look at pictures of early ecumenical meetings, constitutive meetings of the World Council of Churches and of the National Council of the Churches of Christ in the U.S.A., we would see few women. The picture looks different today. But we still struggle to embody a renewed community of women and men. Most leadership positions in congregations and denominations as well as in ecumenical councils are still filled by men.

During the Ecumenical Decade we are challenged to become more intentional about how we form new understandings of unity and new visions of community. Although events such as the ordination of Barbara Harris change the landscape of the ecumenical movement, we cannot assume that the significant change promised by the event will be embodied. Indeed, one of the most essential matters before us during the decade may be ecumenical formation, the act of reading the signs of the times and of creatively incorporating the reality of renewal into our ecumenical understanding and living. Women's struggle to bring down the barriers of race, sex, and class that block renewed community for all God's people is a sign of the times which is critical for the whole creation.

The Ecumenical Decade, in other words, is part of a wider vision, a vision for the whole creation groaning in travail for transformation. The whole creation is awaiting a community that is not exploitative and not oppressive. The integrity of God's creation—with its well-balanced gifts and graces—is essential for a world in which the tree of peace that is rooted in justice will bear fruit.

Before we look at ways in which the Ecumenical Decade is coming to life around the world, I want to recall the way by which we have come to the time. Women's struggle is not new to the ecumenical movement. It has deep roots in the life of the World Council of Churches. Already at the First Assembly of the World Council of Churches in Amsterdam in 1948, delegates received a report on the role and status of women, a report that reflected women's experience in fifty-eight countries.[2] This report, prepared by Sarah Chakko of the Syrian Orthodox Church in India, gave rise to the Commission on the Life and Work of Women. Later, with the leadership of Madeleine Barot, the Department on Cooperation of Men and Women in Church and Society carried the work forward. In the early 1970s the torch was passed to Brigalia Bam of South Africa. In 1974 she convened a landmark consultation that named sexism as sin.[3] This consultation in turn gave rise to the Community of Women and Men in the Church Study, co-sponsored by the Commission on Faith and Order and the Sub-unit on Women in Church and Society. In 1978, as the study process began, an invitation went to local groups to study together and to report their reflections. The study process culminated at an international conference in 1981. At this conference, an understanding of the "web of oppression" matured. Racism, sexism, and classism were seen to be linked together in "a demonic symphony of oppression."[4]

These years of work began to bear fruit at the 1981 meeting of the Central Committee of the World Council of Churches. Meeting in Dresden, the Central Committee affirmed the principle of equal participation for women and men and took action

2. *Revised Interim Report of a Study on the Life and Work of Women in the Churches, Including Reports of an Ecumenical Conference of Church Women, Baarn, Holland, and of the Committee on "The Life and Work of Women in the Church" of the Assembly of the World Council of Churches, Amsterdam, 1948* (Geneva: World Council of Churches, 1948).

3. See *Sexism in the 1970s: Discrimination against Women: Report of a World Council of Churches Consultation, West Berlin, 1974* (Geneva: World Council of Churches, 1975).

4. *The Community of Women and Men in the Church: The Sheffield Report,* ed. Constance F. Parvey (Geneva: World Council of Churches, 1983), p. 145.

to assure the representative composition of all decision-making bodies of the World Council.[5] In 1985, the Central Committee urged member churches of the World Council to "eliminate teachings and practices that discriminate against women."[6] In 1987, the Central Committee conceived the Ecumenical De-cade of the Churches in Solidarity with Women as a response to the United Nations Decade and as a follow-up to the study entitled *The Community of Women and Men in the Church*.[7]

As the Ecumenical Decade comes to life around the world, we hear stories revealing the wide diversity of women's struggle. The National Council of Churches in Kenya has identified issues such as the meeting of women's basic needs for water, food, fuel, and firewood. The Ecumenical Decade committee in South Africa is challenging Christian women to acknowledge their unique role in the struggle to transform South African society. Women are being called to abandon their positions of passivity and servitude, and their strength and resilience for the struggle are being confirmed. The Board of Theological Educa-tion for seminaries in India is asking women to address the question of what can be done in their colleges during the decade. In response, women are challenging seminaries to re-cruit and admit more women as full-time students and to in-troduce women's studies departments. Bishops in the Church of North India and in the Tamil Evangelical Lutheran Church have been writing pastoral letters to correct traditional teach-ings that have kept women from fully participating in their churches. Korean women theologians have issued a statement

5. See *World Council of Churches Central Committee, Minutes of the Thirty-Third Meeting, Dresden, German Democratic Republic, 16-26 August 1981* (Geneva: World Council of Churches, 1981).

6. *World Council of Churches Central Committee, Minutes of the Thirty-Seventh Meeting, Buenos Aires, Argentina, 28 July–8 August 1985* (Geneva: World Council of Churches, 1985), p. 57.

7. *World Council of Churches Central Committee, Minutes of the Thirty-Eighth Meeting, Geneva, Switzerland, 16-24 January 1987* (Geneva: World Council of Churches, 1987), pp. 69-71.

in which they make the connection between Korean national division and the patriarchal culture of domination. They call women and men to stand together before God as the partners we were created to be. Philippine women are focusing their attention on issues facing rural women, particularly the conditions in which women farm and plantation workers live. In Sweden, the priorities for the Ecumenical Decade include collaborating with migrant and refugee women as well as addressing critical issues—violence against women, genetics and reproductive technologies, and the nomination of women to church-governance bodies. When the decade was launched in Costa Rica, Guayumie Indian women traveled eighteen hours to participate in the inauguration proceedings. Men and children are also getting involved. Everywhere women want their children to be fed. Everywhere women want their sons, brothers, husbands, and fathers to be free from the threat of war. Everywhere women of color witness to the double oppression of racism and sexism. Everywhere women call for the end of oppression and for the wholeness of God's people.

Despite the high visibility of women's issues, it has been difficult to launch the Ecumenical Decade in the United States. A lethargy about women's issues lingers following the achievements of the last two decades. It seems especially difficult to focus on the *churches* as agents of change. Women have borne the burden of our struggle against subordination for so long that it is hard to turn to the churches for change. But the decade is about women in solidarity with women. The decade calls the churches to overcome discriminatory teachings and practices that have prevented women's full participation. The decade calls the churches to create a renewed community of women and men, a community of mutual empowerment for the sake of challenging oppression in the global community.

Despite the inertia in the United States, there are nonetheless signs that the Ecumenical Decade is coming to life here in churches and ecumenical bodies. The Evangelical Lutheran

Church in America, the Episcopal Church, the United Methodist Church, the United Church of Christ, the Christian Church (Disciples of Christ), the Church of the Brethren, the African Methodist Episcopal Church, the American Baptist Church, and the Christian Methodist Episcopal Church have as churches adopted as official resolutions the goals of the Ecumenical Decade. Councils of churches are beginning to develop plans for implementing the decade in local communities.

These signs of life notwithstanding, many still ask whether or not the Ecumenical Decade will take hold in the United States, whether or not any real change can result from the activities of the decade. Another question, one raised by both enthusiastic supporters and suspicious bystanders, is how we will know if progress has been made. Will there be a woman head of communion? Will another woman be the General Secretary of the National Council of Churches? Will women become "tall steeple" pastors? Will half the governing boards of congregations and denominations be chaired by women? Will women of color have their place of leadership in the churches and councils? Will churches be on the forefront of the fight for quality day-care and the fight against the frightening feminization of poverty?

We often focus on such signs of change because they are readily visible and verifiable. But I think there is something more basic that must happen if the Ecumenical Decade is really to have a formative role in the churches and in the ecumenical movement. The decade must challenge women and men to consider what the "feminization" of the church may mean for the future life of the church.

But these changes will not be enough to renew the community of women and men. Women painfully confess that the mere presence of women in church and council positions does not change the oppressive structures. This confession brings me back to the recognition that ecumenical formation is one of the most essential matters for the decade. The conjunction of this confession and this recognition reveal another critical focus for our attention during the decade: leadership. I believe it is particularly important to pay attention to women's unique style of leadership as a resource for forming—through redemption and renewal—a new community of women and men.

Women's style of leadership is relational, connectional, flexible, intimate, and passionate as well as nonhierarchical and holistic in perspective. The authority of our style flows from cooperation rather than subordination or domination. Fredrica Harris Thompsett's writings on a theology of intimacy have been very helpful to me as I have attempted to articulate my thinking about leadership style. I note my indebtedness as a way of saying that women's style is also marked by the open sharing of ideas. We know that in such open sharing the most creative, innovative ideas emerge. We know that many viewpoints are better than any one viewpoint. I want to reflect more fully on four of the characteristics that define women's style of leadership.

First, women's style is at its core relational. Mary Hunt of the women-church movement has said, "Our sense of self is organized around being able to make and sustain relationships rather than based on self enhancement through projects, careers or achievements."[8] This sense of self contrasts sharply with the predominant mode of masculine selfhood in our society. Churches now struggling with identity and spiritual depth could be helped by finding and drawing on women's sense of self, which has been lost as a resource for renewal. A relational style values people and process. Such a relational style is especially critical in the ecumenical movement, because ecumenism depends upon nurturing relationships. Ecumenical decision-making is enabled and enhanced as these relationships are tended.

Women's style of leadership is also connectional. It is not

8. Hunt, *Christian Century,* 10 May 1989, p. 493.

dualistic. Our style embodies our understanding that the interdependence of all people in the global village is no longer a
luxury. The nuclear threat, the environmental crisis, and the
distribution of resources make this interdependence imperative
for our survival. We need people with a connectional style of
leadership to build networks and to use these networks to
accomplish goals too ambitious for any one organization. The
ability to make connections is key for ecumenical organization
and understanding. Women's ways of handling the power of
horizontal connectedness can enable the ecumenical movement to embody unity without diminishing the richness of diversity. Women's ways of making connections can enable the
embodiment of the ecumenical vision wherein each and every
person brings gifts to the common table.

Women's style of leadership is also flexible, full of creativity
and imagination. Flexibility is extremely important; indeed,
Leonardo Boff has identified flexibility as a basic category of
biblical theology: "God was infinitely flexible toward humanity,
accepting its reality with its undeniable limitations and onerous
ambiguities. The resulting church clothed itself in a courageous
flexibility toward the Greeks, the Romans and Barbarians, accepting their languages, customs, rituals and religious expressions. It did not demand any more than faith in Jesus Christ."

Flexibility does not mean that "anything goes." Flexibility
is not merely tolerating difference but valuing it. Bigotry and
prejudice flow from frightened, inflexible styles of leadership.
The open, accepting, imaginative, creative capacities of flexible
leadership are critical for renewing community.

Finally, women's style of leadership is intimate and
passionate. For too long women have been accused of being too
emotional, of letting our emotions rule our lives, and (implicitly)
of stunting the rational side of ourselves. But in these times, as
we seek to redeem and renew community, women's ability to
be intimate and passionate will be an asset. Indeed, if we seek

solidarity with those who suffer, we will fail without the fire of our passion and the fuel of intimacy.

Leadership may emerge at the forefront of the discussion of ecumenical formation during the Ecumenical Decade. Unless we are willing to address leadership issues and imagine new styles of leadership, the future for churches, for the ecumenical movement, and for the whole creation looks fraught with great grief. Women can lead the way. Women can be the teachers and prophets in forging a new way of being and doing. "Behold, I am doing a new thing; now it springs forth, do you not perceive it?" (Isa. 43:19).

Ecumenical Leadership:
Power and Women's Voices

Kathleen S. Hurty

T HE goal is to create community," said Maxine Clark Beech, Executive Director of the Scarritt Bennett Center in Nashville. This recently elected leader was knee-deep in newness, helping an organization make a new beginning while being careful about traditions worth preserving. Selecting staff, supervising carpenters and caretakers, shaping a program, creating a team sense among the employees—these were the tasks that were challenging her when she took time out to talk with me about her views on leadership.

"To create community in an organization," she continued, "you need an egalitarian model where each person develops awareness about other jobs, respects the work of others, and affirms the unique contribution of each to the whole." Beech works to stimulate a circle of involvement in ministry, nurturing the commitment required to make it work. While she recognizes that egalitarian models produce uncertainty for some in church

---

Kathleen S. Hurty is Assistant General Secretary of the NCC's Commission on Regional and Local Ecumenism. She is a member of the Evangelical Lutheran Church in America.

leadership, she feels that for too long the church has borrowed hierarchical models from business rather than exploring other theologically sound styles.

For this leader, key elements of the center's work are hospitality and community. As the staff works together in a group that follows this model of leadership, they are finding out what it means to be open to each other, to be candid, to work together on problem-solving, to be hospitable. While she recognizes these elements as ideals, Beech believes that it is essential—albeit risky—to explore ways to move toward such ideals. At the Scarritt Bennett Center, she is taking the risk of developing programs to assist the church in exploring difficult issues and new themes.

In Beech's view, power is an unlimited resource: there is enough of it for everyone. To look at power in this way creates a climate in which people can use their creative energies to the fullest. Rather than putting the emphasis on control, Beech chooses to emphasize creativity and commitment.

This is the voice of one leader who is a woman. By virtue of her calling, she calls the church to be in solidarity with women who are modeling new styles of leadership. She is one of many creative women leaders, standing as a sentinel and a symbol of opportunity as the church looks for leaders for the twenty-first century.

As Maxine Clark Beech recognizes, leadership is central to life in community. When people work or worship or make decisions about life together, leadership is either called forth or emerges as essential. Yet today there is increasing concern about what is called "a crisis of leadership." We decry the loss of "great" leaders in public service, in the private sector, in churches, and in the ecumenical movement. We look for leaders who can bring to their work a combination of authority, integrity, compassion, and wisdom, but we find few who possess all these characteristics. Accordingly, attitudes toward leaders are frequently fractious. Perspectives on leadership are also beginning to change and will continue to change as we move toward the coming century.

Churches, like other institutions and organizations, count on leaders to inspire and guide their mission and ministry to fulfillment. Churches call leaders into service by ordaining priests and ministers and pastors, by consecrating missionaries, church-school teachers, and deacons, and by electing bishops, executives, and church-council and committee chairpersons. Churches also call leaders to serve in daily life, for the churches as *ecclesia,* as "called out people," are also churches at work in the world. But churches, like other institutions and organizations, have taken leadership for granted and have not considered the concept of leadership.

In this chapter I will consider the concept of leadership and seek scriptural sources for a renewed connection between leadership and power. At every point I will introduce women's voices raised in the quest for a new vision of leadership at this critical juncture between the centuries. It is my hope that these refreshed perspectives on leadership will challenge the churches to take seriously the issue of solidarity with women in leadership. Additionally, I want to point out that, by drawing on scriptural sources and delving into rich religious traditions seeded by seldom-studied experiences of women in leadership, the churches can contribute significantly to discussions of leadership that are going on globally. In conclusion, I will suggest some specific ways in which women and men working together ecumenically can recreate the lively art of leadership.

Leadership: A Multifaceted Concept

The exercise of leadership is shaped by the language we use to refer to it. The Oxford English Dictionary defines leadership as the "dignity, office or position of a leader" and as "the ability to lead." And the OED says that "to lead" is "to conduct," "to accompany," "to show the way," "to guide by going in advance." There are many other ways of talking about leadership; different dimensions of leadership may be seen through different lenses. What follows are four different perspectives on leadership.

First, leadership in organizations can be viewed as an aspect of management. Management textbooks refer to leadership as the functions necessary to induce followers to work toward given goals representing the needs, wants, aspirations, and expectations of both leaders and followers.[1] This view of leadership emphasizes its functional or technical dimension and minimizes its relational dimension. Feminists are among those seeking to articulate a more holistic view of leadership, a view that accents the interactive character of leadership, which is mutual empowerment.[2]

Second, leadership is related to organizational power. Since power is very often construed as power over people and resources, persons in leadership are perceived to be those who have power over others. But this view of leadership perpetuates a domination-subordination hierarchy. Feminists are also seeking to widen the narrow perception of power that shapes such patterns, suggesting patterns for exercising power with other persons.[3]

1. See James McGregor Burns, *Leadership* (New York: Harper & Row, 1978).

2. See Kathy E. Ferguson, *The Feminist Case against Bureaucracy* (Philadelphia: Temple University Press, 1984), and several works by Rosabeth Moss Kanter: *Men and Women of the Corporation* (New York: Basic Books, 1977); "Power Failure in Management Circuits," *Harvard Business Review* (July-Aug. 1979); "Power, Leadership, and Participatory Management," *Theory into Practice* 20 (Fall 1981); and *When Giants Learn to Dance: Mastering the Challenges of Strategy, Management, and Careers in the 1990s* (New York: Simon & Schuster, 1989).

3. See Jane Mansbridge, *Beyond Adversary Democracy* (New York: Basic Books, 1980); Elizabeth Janeway, *Powers of the Weak* (New York: Alfred A. Knopf, 1980); and Carol Gilligan, *In a Different Voice: Psychological Theory and Women's Development* (Cambridge, Mass.: Harvard University Press, 1982).

Third, leadership is an ecclesiological as well as a sociological concept. Sociologically speaking, leaders lead by virtue of the position they hold in an organization or institution. Leadership is part of the network of power within organizational and institutional life, informed by beliefs about how people do and should live and work together. Ecclesiologically, leadership is informed by beliefs about God and the nature of the church. The church as the body of Christ, as constituted by the Holy Spirit, as the community of the baptized—the church is not simply an organization or institution in sociological terms. Leadership within church structures, therefore, calls for unique consideration, the kind in which a number of churches are engaging by undertaking major studies on ministry. The Ecumenical Decade challenges churches to reconceive language about leadership so that the consequently renewed exercise of leadership in the church will be more fully shared by women and men.[4]

Fourth, and finally, leadership may be viewed as both formal and informal. Churches, for example, choose leaders with care and often through the formal processes of ordination or consecration or election. But leaders may also emerge informally in churches, particularly in those contexts in which volunteers contribute to church activities. Indeed, volunteers are a rich resource for churches and for the ecumenical movement, as groups like Church Women United show: significant ecumenical leadership has emerged from its work with women volun-

4. As resources for this reconception, see the following: Letty Russell, *The Future of Partnership* (Philadelphia: Westminster Press, 1979), and *Household of Freedom: Authority in Feminist Theology* (Philadelphia: Westminster/John Knox Press, 1987); Sallie McFague, *Metaphorical Theology: Models of God in Religious Language* (Philadelphia: Fortress Press, 1982), and *Models of God: Theology for an Ecological Nuclear Age* (Philadelphia: Fortress Press, 1987); Elisabeth Schüssler Fiorenza, *In Memory of Her: A Feminist Theological Reconstruction of Christian Origins* (New York: Crossroad, 1983); and Rosemary Radford Ruether, *Women-Church: Theology and Practice of Feminist Liturgical Communities* (San Francisco: Harper & Row, 1985).

teers. In the face of such developments, churches are challenged to be more intentional about the contribution of volunteers.[5]

These diverse perspectives on leadership are but starting points for discussions in which we need to broaden our conception of leadership. For the leadership crisis of which we speak is connected at least in part to the limited notions of leadership with which we live and work. Particularly during the Ecumenical Decade, churches are called to enrich their understanding and exercise of leadership by appreciating the experience and expertise unique to women in leadership.

Scriptural Starting Points

Churches are endowed with rich resources that they can draw on as they answer this call. The stories of women in Scripture offer delightfully creative possibilities for refreshed views of leadership. There are the stories of Deborah the judge, of Huldah the prophet, of Esther the policy advocate who intervened on behalf of her people, of Ruth the care-giver across cultural boundaries, of Junia the apostle (Rom. 16:7), and of Phoebe, who exercised the functions of a bishop. Feminist biblical scholarship enables us to engage these women stories as sources for models of renewed leadership.[6]

Mary's Magnificat also offers a remarkable model for leadership. I discovered this resource during the Marian Year while I was preparing a paper for the International Ecumenical Conference entitled "Mary: Woman for All Christians." Since I had

5. See Marlene Wilson, *How to Mobilize Church Volunteers* (Minneapolis: Augsburg Publishing House, 1983).

6. See, for example, Phyllis Trible, *God and the Rhetoric of Sexuality* (Philadelphia: Fortress Press, 1978), and *Texts of Terror: Literary-Feminist Readings of Biblical Narratives* (Philadelphia: Fortress Press, 1984); Elisabeth Moltmann-Wendel, *The Women around Jesus* (New York: Paulist Press, 1977); and Elisabeth Schüssler Fiorenza, *In Memory of Her*.

been asked to reflect on Mary from my perspective as a Lutheran woman, I turned to Luther's treatise on the Magnificat. To my delight I discovered that his treatise is essentially a treatise on governance. In this regard, it is first of all noteworthy that Luther addressed his treatise to his "Serene Highness, Prince John Frederick, Duke of Saxony" and declared at the outset that this "sacred hymn of the most blessed Mother of God" is to be "learned and kept in mind by all who would rule well and be helpful lords."[7] Moreover, Luther's appreciation of Mary's model is based on an appreciation of her experience: "Bear in mind that the Blessed Virgin Mary is speaking on the basis of her own experience, in which she was enlightened and instructed by the Holy Spirit."[8] And Luther heard Mary saying that God's mercy rather than God's strength is God's first and noblest work. God's mercy is extended to all who are willing to be poor in spirit, to be bare before God and others.[9] Power from this perspective, wrote Luther, is hidden in powerlessness and weakness. Precisely in his powerlessness, Christ accomplished his mightiest act.[10] Through the voice of Mary, therefore, Luther laid out a view of governance that at once challenges the rich and powerful and uplifts the poor and ordinary.

Women on Power: Critique and Creativity

Taking Luther's lead, let us continue to consider Mary's model for leadership. Hers is a model marked by her experience of poverty, her willingness to be vulnerable, her deliberation and decision-making, her reliance on the Holy Spirit, her doubt, and her delight. These are marks of partnership. Partnership

7. Martin Luther, "The Sermon on the Mount and the Magnificat," in *Luther's Works,* vol. 21, ed. Jaroslav Pelikan (St. Louis: Concordia, 1958).

8. Ibid., p. 299.

9. Ibid., p. 339.

10. Ibid., p. 340.

with God and with one another, as modeled by Mary, is the pattern of leadership to which we all—men and women alike— are called.

Partnership with God and with one another excludes the practices of domination and subordination. God's mercy is not passed down from a hierarchical pinnacle but bestowed by God's presence with us where we are. Letty Russell uses the biblical metaphor of God as Housekeeper of all creation when she talks about authority: "Like the woman searching high and low for the lost coin, God continues to search throughout her world house (the oikoumene) looking for all the outcasts and lost persons of society and rejoicing when they are found."[11] These words describe the perspective and posture of partnership.

Mary's model also points to partnership as mutual empowerment—specifically to five elements of empowerment.

The first element is collaboration for change. Mary, woman of power, gave birth to Jesus. By giving birth, Mary accomplished the work God had asked her to do. Open to the mysterious, grace-filled message of the Holy Spirit, Mary thereby chose to allow God to work within her body and her being. Mary's choice can speak to each of us about power as creative collaboration with God, for God calls each of us to be collaborators with our bodies and our beings.

The second element of empowerment is nurtured growth. Mary, woman of power, breast-fed God. Understanding nurturance as power, Mary called for care of the poor, the oppressed, the downtrodden. She identified with these people.[12] From a patriarchal perspective, nurturance is women's work. But the image of power as nurturance is not gender-specific. Women have breasts and wombs and thus have unique responsibilities for the nurturance of children. But, more fundamentally, nur-

11. Russell, *Household of Freedom.*
12. See *Mary in the New Testament*, ed. Raymond E. Brown et al. (Philadelphia: Fortress Press, 1978).

turance is a responsibility of partnership. It is a way of caring
not only for children but also for the suffering, the weary, the
hungry, the homeless—all *God's* children. Mary's model offers
us the opportunity to see the need for nurturant power as a part
of leadership in all arenas of life.

The third element of empowerment is emotional energy.
Mary, woman of power, sang—at once crying and celebrating.
Mary's expression of emotion evidences the power of emotional
energy. Tears of compassion, tears of righteous anger, tears of
shared joy—all are sources of power. Mary's model for leadership leads us to work in offices or parish boardrooms in ways
that stir up passion for justice, acknowledge a hurting sister or
brother, or celebrate accomplishment. By expressing our emotional energy, we are carrying out a central responsibility of
leadership: the creation of community.

The fourth element of empowerment is pondered mutuality.
Mary, woman of power, pondered God's actions in her life,
taking account of her son, her kinfolk, and her community.
Mary can teach us about the power of deep reflection on the
human relationships that are part of our world. Indeed, from
Mary we can learn the power of pondered mutuality. Taking
into account not only the wider world but also our personal
inner world and the community in which we live strengthens
the perspective from which we think and plan as leaders. It is
the practice of partnership in leadership.

The fifth element of empowerment is reciprocal talk. Mary,
woman of power, spoke God's justice when she saw the depths
of human misery and need. Mary can teach us about the power
of reciprocal talk. We can learn from her how to hear the other
when we speak, how to listen to the vulnerable ones, how to
share our own pain and joy. We can learn from her how to speak
for peace with justice and for justice with peace. We can learn
from her how to work at conflict resolution, a form of reciprocal
talk. Contemporary metaphors of this powerful reciprocity include Mary, Mother of the Streets; Mary, Mother of the Disap-

peared; and Mary, Mother of the Oppressed. A new iconography of leadership, embracing reciprocity as well as mutuality, is coming to life.

Mary's model of partnership as mutual empowerment embodies both an ethic of caring and an ethic of justice.[13] In this model, reason and emotion are balanced; wholeness and connectedness are central values. These, along with the elements of empowerment, enable the shift from power exercised from a dominant-subordinate posture to power exercised in partnership.

A Proposal and Priorities for the 1990s

To provide an opportunity for identifying leadership patterns appropriate for the coming century, I propose a leadership project with wide participation. As I envision it, this project would embrace four significant sub-projects.

First, the project would involve seminary-sponsored roundtable discussions that would bring diverse groups of people together to draw from their own deep wells of experience in ecumenical leadership. These groups would also reflect on Scripture, Christian tradition, and church history, always alert to fresh perspectives on power and leadership. Other resources for reflection could include current thinking on an ecclesiology of community[14] and on "koinonia" as a "meta-model" for ecumenical community.[15]

Second, the project would involve a major consultation on ecumenical leadership. The consultation would draw together

13. For a discussion of an ethic of caring and an ethic of justice, see Carol Gilligan, *In a Different Voice*.

14. See Elizabeth Johnson, "The Symbolic Character of Theological Statements about Mary," *Journal of Ecumenical Studies* 22 (Spring 1985).

15. See Emmanuel Sullivan, "Koinonia as a Meta-Model for Future Church Unity," *Ecumenical Trends* 18 (Jan. 1989).

representatives of the diverse roundtable discussions, representatives of churches, and theologians. The purpose of the
consultation would be to gather the insights of the group and
develop a model of leadership to be tested in a variety of
communities by both experienced leaders and up-and-coming
leaders of the next generation.

From the work of this consultation would come the third
part of the project: curriculum development. Materials for seminary courses as well as congregational resources could be prepared. Empowerment teams for the formation of ecumenical
leadership could be trained to nurture ongoing efforts, to become mentors for a new generation of leaders, and to assist in
the placement of potential leaders.

Fourth, the project would involve developing an "ecumenical career service." This service, which would be committed to
an enlarged and inclusive talent-pool accounting for all aspects
of empowering leadership styles, could match needs for ecumenical leadership with individuals having unique gifts and
graces as leaders. The ongoing development of professional
leadership would also be a responsibility of this service.

What would enable this proposed project to become reality?
One dream for the Ecumenical Decade is to ask each member
church of the World Council of Churches to act on its solidarity
with women by funding or seconding a person to work on this
leadership project for three years. This person would have primary
responsibility for collaborating with staff from other churches in
organizing the roundtable discussions, the consultation, the curriculum development, and the ecumenical career service.

What are the problems with the proposed project? Some
will see the proposal as a process that is too slow, too unwieldy
when it comes to global coordination, and too focused on education rather than action. From my perspective, however, effective work on the transformation of ecumenical leadership
must be widely participatory and will take time. Global coordination is crucial but need not be unwieldy with the telecom-

munications technology of today. And it must be remembered that education *is* action. People learn by doing. And the process of developing models of mutually empowering ecumenical leadership is also action. Other critics will see the project as too costly or will suggest that funds would be better spent on other work. My response? Certainly the proposal is costly, and funds can always be used in multiple ways. But the articulation and development of collaborative, caring, creative ecumenical leadership by the churches in solidarity with women will serve a very significant need. For, without such leadership, the ministry and mission of the churches as well as of the ecumenical movement will be rudderless.

The formation of ecumenical leadership for the future must be high on the list of priorities for the 1990s. Key issues involved in the formation of leadership, issues that need to be explored, are these: women's styles of leadership and their significance for ecumenical life; the relationship of style to concepts of authority, integrity, and unity; the ethical underpinnings of ecumenical leadership; the church as a community of moral deliberation and the qualities of leadership called for in such a community; leadership in the global context, with particular attention paid to perspectives on leadership from a variety of cultures; conflict resolution, transformation, and leadership.

These issues are further illumined by Rosabeth Moss Kanter, Professor of Business Administration at the Harvard Business School. She identifies thirteen new demands on leadership for these changing times:

1. creating a more flexible image of a leader, an image that looks beyond the male model;
2. searching for leadership in new and even unexpected places, especially by encouraging leadership talent in people who have been outside the mainstream;
3. managing decline and expectations in institutions with smaller growth;

4. managing in the face of a less controllable environment;
5. holding together fragmented constituencies;
6. satisfying multiple stakeholders;
7. giving constituency a greater voice;
8. designing less stratified, more responsive systems;
9. sharing leadership;
10. weighing more data and seeking information from more sources;
11. changing the role of leaders from one of ordering to one of inspiring;
12. handling greater risks;
13. restoring faith in the legitimacy and efficacy of large institutions.[16]

Churches would do well to consider these issues and demands and to turn them into opportunities for the formation of creative ecumenical leadership. The choice we can make to consider these and other issues is momentous. Both the ecumenical movement and the churches stand at a critical juncture, one at which we must recognize that leadership formation is foundational for the future.

---

16. See Kanter, "Power, Leadership, and Participatory Management."

Still In But Out

Eileen W. Lindner

IN 1973, Elizabeth Howell Verdesi published *In But Still Out*, a chronicle of power twice won and lost by women in one communion noteworthy for its ecumenical commitments.[1] Verdesi reviewed the history of participation of Presbyterian women in their church during the first seventy-five years of this century. She concluded that, while women during those years achieved ecclesiastical equality, were recognized as professionally trained, and were given significant responsibility in both lay and clergy roles, they continued to deal uncomfortably and ineffectively with power within the church. She described this situation as one of being *in* but still *out* of the central currents of the church.[2]

Nearly a decade and a half later, we are able to observe considerable progress in the role and status of women within

1. Verdesi, *In But Still Out* (Philadelphia: Westminster Press, 1973).
2. Ibid., p. 181.

Eileen W. Lindner is Associate General Secretary for Ecumenical Relationships in the NCC. A church historian, she is a member of the Presbyterian Church, U.S.A.

the church. Nevertheless, we may conclude that a form of marginalization continues to describe the circumstance of many women in the church. Among the tasks to be taken up during the Ecumenical Decade is an evaluation of the ecumenical development of processes that lead to the fuller reception of the church as a community of women and men. Moreover, the progress of such integration will be measured not only by the role and status of women within the ecumenical movement but, more significantly, by the incorporation of the insights of feminism into the methodology, community life, and organizational styles of the ecumenical movement.

At the heart of the ecumenical movement is the impulse for the unity of the church, with an acknowledged appropriate diversity. While the reign of Christ with the abiding presence of the Spirit may be affirmed, an authentic structural embodiment of the church of Jesus Christ remains elusive. Theological convergence, even when it is developed on central issues, is not enough. A paradox long observed within the ecumenical movement is that the *expressions* of theological truths which are held in common can themselves become new sources of division. It is precisely this riddle of Christian unity, along with the churches' persistent perpetuation of it, that prompted Karl Barth to speak of every division as a *scandal*.[3]

The obstacles to such unity are themselves diverse: they are often as sociological, economic, cultural, or psychological at their root as they are historical, theological, or ecclesiological in origin. Yet another irony of the process of ecumenical development is that, in their turn, many of these "obstacles" to unity can serve as rich catalysts for ecumenical formation. The role and status of women and in particular the ordination of women may prove to be examples of just such a paradigm of ecumenical development.

3. Barth, *Church Dogmatics*, VI/1, ed. G. W. Bromiley and T. F. Torrance (Edinburgh: T. & T. Clark, 1957), p. 675.

In the postwar era, contemporary conciliar ecumenism most often apprehended the questions of the role and status of women through the larger and somewhat refracting prism of the "participation of the laity." This focus on the distinction between clergy and laity obscured the question of gender inclusiveness behind a concern to avoid clericalism. The report from the Committee on the Life and Work of Women in the Church at the First Assembly of the World Council of Churches in Amsterdam in 1948 lifted up the training of the laity as a central task of ecumenical development.[4] Not until 1963 did the Commission on Faith and Order of the World Council undertake a study entitled "Concerning the Ordination of Women."

Ecumenism, particularly in its conciliar expression, has celebrated the rise of lay movements during the last four decades. Despite this history, such ecumenical efforts have achieved only an awkward and uneasy accord with the established women's organizations within member communions. This is partly attributable to the complexities of polity and to respect for the ecclesiological integrity of the communions within the governance of church councils. Such explanations are not entirely convincing, however, and the existence of *independent* ecumenical women's organizations such as Church Women United in the United States admit of a more complex and troubled history in relation to ecumenical councils.

Madeleine Barot, long a leader of World Council work to enhance the role and status of women, has perennially called on the council to increase self-critical reflection on this particular segment of the laity within the ecumenical movement. The Ecumenical Decade offers opportunities for this very thing. It also offers an opportunity for reconsidering the history of ecumenical development and the part played by traditional women's

4. Hanfried Kruger, "Significance of the Three Assemblies," in *The Ecumenical Advance, 1948-1968*, vol. 2 of *A History of the Ecumenical Movement*, ed. Harold Fey (London: SPCK, 1970), p. 38.

organizations. No sincere effort at church unity, much less at church union, can long exclude such an exploration.

If the inclusion of traditional women's organizations within conciliar ecumenical structures has been fraught with difficulties, the debate over the ordination of women promised to be fractious. But, despite these early dire predictions, this debate has continued to generate almost as much light as heat. The questions surrounding the ordination of women have engendered conversations within and among churches that have paid dividends by forging a greater consensus on the subject of the practice of ministry.

In 1980, Connie Parvey edited a document produced by the World Council's Commission on Faith and Order that includes an excellent bibliography along with an enduring survey of the ecumenical spectrum concerning the ordination of women.[5] Even the most cursory reading of this document convinces one that no facile concessions—theological or practical—will do. This document also identifies the central significance of this issue for the ecumenical movement. It makes it clear that the practice of ministry which precludes the full participation of women and men together is "an act of disunity against humankind."[6] This fundamental issue of human disunity nags below the surface of the issue of women's ordination. Sexism at the point of origin of gender-related acts of disunity, then, emerges as a critical stumbling-block to all forms of unity.

From the unique multilateral discussion of church union, the Consultation on Church Union (COCU), came a sober assessment of the consequences of the debilitating and polarizing sexism that has been embodied in church hermeneutics, liturgy,

5. *Ordination of Women in Ecumenical Perspective,* Faith and Order Paper No. 105, ed. Constance F. Parvey (Geneva: World Council of Churches, 1980). For a useful and thorough review of women's issues in the World Council of Churches, see Ans J. Van der Bent, *Vital Ecumenical Concerns* (Geneva: World Council of Churches, 1986), pp. 192-213.

6. *Ordination of Women in Ecumenical Perspective,* p. 37.

theology, and the practice of ministry. The consultation expressed concern that if this problem was not addressed in a substantive way, there would be long-term disunity. It commented, "[The consultation may] discover within five to ten years that many of its members have been so alienated along the way that 'unity' has become a gentleman's agreement within the dominant group, rather than the agreement of partners who have struggled together toward true mutuality."[7] Now, a decade since this statement was made, it is not likely that even the most gentlemanly agreements about unity can be obtained. Ironically, the process of ecumenical development that has occurred in the wake of the first conversations about women's ordination as an obstacle to church unity has given rise to questions about the nature of the ministry itself, questions that may well endure beyond the debate over women's eligibility for ministerial office.

This dynamic is not unique to the debate over women's ordination. It is inherent in the nature of the ecumenical enterprise. Ecumenical advance can be and often is realized precisely in dialogue that surrounds such church-dividing issues. The World Council's Commission on Faith and Order has illustrated this dynamic in its document entitled *Baptism, Eucharist, and Ministry* (BEM), a document that has engendered considerable ecumenical advance by engaging churches around centrally and classically controversial issues.

Churches that received this document were asked to frame "responses" which addressed the utility as well as the content of the document's statements on baptism, the Eucharist, and ministry. By asking for responses to the usefulness of the document for facilitating reflection, for renewing worship life, and for assisting the respective churches in their dialogue with each other, the commission knowingly pressed toward the furtherance of insight. Such a process quickens the readiness for the

7. *In Quest of the Church of Christ Uniting: An Emerging Theological Consensus* (Princeton: Consultation on Church Union, 1980), p. 56.

"reception" of and ultimately the internalization of the insights of one tradition by another. Inherent in this paradigm for ecumenical development is a respect for the maturity and integrity of each tradition as well as an acknowledgment that a new gestalt has not yet been discerned.

A similar process of cognitive development and transformation in spirit may be projected with regard to the issue of women's ordination. Shannon Clarkson, referring particularly to bilateral ecumenical dialogues, writes, "Any chance to address the scandal of particularity ought to be explored. To refuse to discuss an issue is to create yet another scandal and to deny the work of the Holy Spirit. The issue of women's ordination is not an insuperable obstacle. The Spirit may, in fact, speak to one church through the insights of another."[8] The ecumenical urgency of such church-dividing issues endows them with a particular ability to transform centuries-old controversies into contemporary conversations toward common ground.

In a chapter of a festschrift for Philip Potter, Madeleine Barot boldly offers the outlines of a paradigm for ecumenical development with regard to the ordination of women. She writes,

> Many of these questions are disturbing, even annoying, because they are difficult to define and because they are liable to be very far-reaching in their effects. For the moment it [the ordination of women] is perceived as an obstacle on the road to church unity. Perhaps before long it will prove to be an issue which obliges all our churches to re-examine their doctrine and practice of ministry and creates the opportunity for a more honest ecumenical dialogue. . . . We already know now that the unity we long for cannot . . . tolerate the exclusion of anyone on any grounds whatever—race, sex, dogma, tradition.[9]

8. Clarkson, "Steps Toward Unity—A Mutual Recognition of Ordained Ministries," *Journal of Ecumenical Studies*, Summer 1986, p. 482.

9. Barot, "What Do These Women Want?" in *Faith and Faithfulness: Essays on Contemporary Ecumenical Thought*, ed. Pauline Webb (Geneva: World Council of Churches, 1984), p. 83.

Yet even as we glimpse what may become common ground, there are lessons to be drawn from the praxis of the church. For even though the first ordained woman to hold the office of president of the National Council of Churches, U.S.A., has recently completed her term, the question of the reception of women's full participation in the ministry of the church still confronts us at every turn. If we look to the episcopacy, to the academy, to pulpits and parishes, we see evidence in the placement of clergywomen which indicates that even when the way to ordination is open, women often find themselves in but still out. Indeed, at the time of her election as president of the National Council, Reverend Patricia McClurg noted that it is probably easier for a woman to be elected to such an ecumenical office than to be called as a senior pastor of a large congregation.

There are numerous indications of women's ongoing secondary status in the church. Although we may take into consideration the overall lower age of women clergy, as well as cultural and ethnic diversity and the diversity of communions, women clergy are over-represented among part-time, unemployed, and underemployed clergy in the United State. None of the member communions of the National Council lists a woman as "head of communion." Only one lists a woman as "ecumenical officer."[10] And, although the National Council of Churches in the United States has had one lay woman fill the position of general secretary, the World Council of Churches has not yet elected a woman to this office. Further, neither council has called an ordained woman to the office. These indicators suggest that the offices which clearly symbolize the church as church are still beyond the reach of clergywomen as the Ecumenical Decade gets underway.

Nevertheless, although women are still denied the highest posts in ecumenical agencies, they have garnered invaluable

10. *Yearbook of American and Canadian Churches*, ed. Constant H. Jacquet (Nashville: Abingdon Press, 1988).

experiences within the ecumenical movement that are often
denied them in their own communions. Perhaps because councils of churches are not themselves communions, they have
offered women opportunities for leadership development, spiritual and intellectual growth, and skill development. By exercising ecumenical callings, then, women have been able, by the
power of the Spirit, to transcend the ecclesial status quo.

Conciliar ecumenism at all levels—local, regional,
national, and international—has also provided women with
more opportunities for ecumenical leadership development
than have the bilateral dialogues. In bilateral dialogues, experiences of women's ordination are limited and tend to limit
discussion. In conciliar ecumenical contexts, which are characterized by the presence of more partner churches, churches that
have never ordained women can directly encounter churches
that have always ordained women and can do so in ways in
which women's ordination is not, as such, at stake. There is a
resultant willingness to offer leadership positions to women
without ordination being an issue. A challenge facing conciliar
ecumenism is that of communicating these experiences and
insights to member communions. Here, as with *Baptism, Eucharist, and Ministry*, ecumenical development may be an occasion for the renewal of the churches themselves.

The bone and tissue of the ecumenical body is held in place
by this sinew of ecumenical development. Far too few people
are thinking about and nurturing this sinew in the interest of
the whole body. For ecumenical development is not only for
women and about women's issues; it is for and about all individuals and communities on the margin. It is an urgent task
to be undertaken for the sake of Christian unity.

A Vision for Ecumenical Mission: Challenge during the Decade

Mary Motte, F.M.M.

TWO ecumenical documents of the 1980s indicate significant directions for ecumenical mission: *Common Witness* and *Mission and Evangelism: An Ecumenical Affirmation*.[1] Both documents challenge the churches to consider their solidarity with women in the context of the call to mission.

Common Witness, prepared by the Joint Working Group of the World Council of Churches and the Roman Catholic Church, notes the movement toward communion among

1. *Common Witness: A Study Document of the Joint Working Group of the Roman Catholic Church and the World Council of Churches*, World Council Mission Series (Geneva: World Council of Churches, 1982); *Mission and Evangelism: An Ecumenical Affirmation* (New York: Division of Overseas Ministries, NCCC/USA, 1983).

Mary Motte, a Franciscan Missionary of Mary, is Director of the Mission Resource Center for the U.S. province of this religious order. She is the Roman Catholic consultant to the WCC's Commission on World Mission and Evangelism, and a liaison member of the NCC's Commission on Faith and Order representing the U.S. Catholic Mission Association.

women and men, a movement inspired by the Holy Spirit. Through witness, this movement toward communion is extending itself in new communities. Such continual renewal—of spirituality as well as of lifestyle—is the basis for the authentic witness of the church in the world today.

Mission and Evangelism situates the call to mission in the context of the call to ecumenism as well as the call to witness in the world. The document demonstrates considerable convergence on central missiological issues. Among these are the issues of the church and its unity in God's mission, mission in Christ's way, good news to the poor, and witness among peoples of other living faiths.

The movement of the Holy Spirit toward community and the diverse ways in which Christian community is emerging in history are important indicators for the direction of mission today. The movement of the Holy Spirit, to the extent that it is unimpeded, is also directing women and men toward communion and enabling us to live in new ways. These two fruits of the Spirit's movement are interrelated. For the movement of the Spirit that is leading men and women toward communion is particularly present and powerful in Christian communities that have assumed their missionary responsibility.[2]

I want to explore this interrelatedness. More specifically, I want to suggest that, whatever the specific missionary situation, the missionary methods of presence and participation are of primary importance today. Further, I want to suggest that women are uniquely gifted for mission as presence and participation. Like Mary, our prime exemplar, women can creatively interact with the Holy Spirit to bring the world into a new relationship with its Creator.

---

2. See José Comblin, *The Holy Spirit and Liberation* (Maryknoll, N.Y.: Orbis Books, 1989), pp. 7-13, 19-33.

Women's Religious Experience
and the Challenge to Mission

In the wake of women's struggle around the world to continue to be part of the church's mission, more attention has been given to our religious experience. The attention has been focused mainly on our self-reflection, which has led us to move beyond missionary responses appropriate to another time and place. Here I think of women who choose to care for persons dying of AIDS, combining physical care with compassion. I think of women who provide homes and promote dignity for abused women and children. And I think in a special way of a woman who stands with prostitutes to help them experience God's love for them.

This self-reflection has led me to see that the power to knit life together is particularly the gift of women, whether or not we are biological mothers. This knitting together is undergirded by an intuitive sense of wholeness that escapes the estrangement of relegating life-giving reality to neatly delineated categories. Life is sacred. Life is a gift. Life is wholeness; the whole creation is interrelated. For women, all life is potentially a reflection of God the Creator. Our presence to God is also our presence to God in and through all God's creation. Educational systems and societal mind-sets seem to do their best to deny or diminish or distort this innate sense of wholeness that women bear as a gift of God. But there are women who do not suffer this denial or diminishment or distortion. Testifying to this are the "Praises" of Afua Kuma, a farmer and midwife from the Kwawu area of Ghana:

> Yesu, who has received the poor and makes us honorable, our exceedingly wise friend, we depend on you as the tongue depends on the jaw. [You are] the rock. We hide under you, the great bush with cooling shades, the giant tree who enables the climbers to see the heavens.

Yesu, when you walk in the darkness you do not need a lamp. When you step out the sun goes before you and the lightening comes behind you.[3]

And Mary's praise echoes that of her sister Hannah, who preceded her: "My soul proclaims the greatness of the Lord, and my spirit rejoices in God my Savior, because God has looked upon my low estate. Yes, from now onwards all generations will call me blessed, for the Almighty has done great things for me. Holy is God's name" (Luke 1:46-49).

Another gift that women bring to this time for mission is the gift of integrity. The sacrament which communicates this gift of integrity is that of one person's presence to another. In this time we are pressed to a fuller response to this giftedness. One concrete way in which some women are living a fuller response to the gift of integrity is by being a presence to and with people of other living faiths. The question of how to relate to people of other living faiths is one of the most provocative questions in ecumenical discussions today. Stepping aside from the controversy are women who, with a sense of the integrity of their Christian faith and a sense of being called to mission, are living as a presence to and with people of other living faiths. The lifestyles of these women are concrete expressions of respect for their neighbors. These women listen to the stories that their neighbors tell them about life and death, joy and sorrow, and love. At the same time, the way these women live tells the story of Jesus, who came to be among us, who saved us from the oppression of sin, who rose from the dead, and who still lives with us. But these Christian women do not feel called to convert their sisters and brothers of other religious traditions. To do so would be dishonest. It would betray the very basic contract of living together as neighbors in love. It would betray the com-

3. Cited in *With Passion and Compassion: Third World Women Doing Theology,* ed. Virginia Fabella, M.M., and Mercy Amba Oduyoye (Maryknoll, N.Y.: Orbis Books, 1988), p. 42.

mitment to building up a more human and just society. Accordingly, these women simply live with their neighbors. The heart of all their living is simply telling those around them about God's love for everyone.[4] Their intuitive sense of wholeness enables them to integrate genuine respect for the other with gracious faith in Christ; in this way they live out their deepest adoration of the Mystery of God present and active in their midst.

Women also have a particular giftedness for "standing with," for "walking beside"—the stuff of solidarity. This giftedness, a prerequisite for mission, emerges from our experience of being set aside simply because we are women. Structures of church and society make women marginal, even as their overseers profess their commitment *not* to do so. As women undergo conversion, the turning around of our experience of marginalization accompanied by a deep conviction of groundedness in the Creator God, we are empowered for renewing both church and society. This sense of solidarity manifests itself as we become more aware of our networks—our "tough-spun webs"—with sisters around the world.

This sense of solidarity makes us aware of our own tremendous resiliency, illustrated for me by women in an encampment of landless people in southern Brazil. When the encampment began, there were about one thousand families. After six months, because of the difficult living conditions, only eight hundred were still there. Many of the women I met were married and mothers of several children. These women welcomed me warmly. When I asked about their lives as women, they responded enthusiastically, saying that they were totally committed together with the men to building up the village. I witnessed the embodiment of their commitment as I watched them carry heavy sacks of grain slung over their shoulders, just like the men. These

4. See Luise Ahrens, M.M., "Option for the Poor: Missionaries in Solidarity," unpublished public lecture given at the Mission Resource Center, Franciscan Missionaries of Mary, Northern Providence, Rhode Island, 13 Apr. 1989.

women were also among the leaders of the village. When I asked
the women what their greatest difficulty was, they quickly responded, "The double day." By this they meant the tasks related
to children, housing, and food—tasks additional to those they
shared with the men, tasks the men did not share with them.
These women were indeed representatives of resiliency.

The experience of being on the margin, which may give
rise to the sense of solidarity, is most of all the experience of
the poor. Now poor women are joining hands. They are falling
into step with all those who struggle and suffer discrimination
and injustice. The significance of these solidarity movements is
manifest as these poor women become symbols with dynamic
power. As I see their solidarity with all who struggle and suffer,
I think of the countless women crying for their children destroyed by nuclear abuse in the Pacific. I think of the mothers
who mourn their daughters and sons who had visions of a new
world but who were crushed by unredeeming and unredeemable
power. I think also of the four North American women who
suffered martyrdom in El Salvador. I think about how the humil-
iation of their deaths was due to their solidarity with the people
of El Salvador. And I think about how these women have
become a glorious memory that gives continual strength and
new courage to the people today.

Signs of Missiological Openings to Solidarity with Women

The World Conference on Mission and Evangelism that was
held in San Antonio, Texas, in 1989 raised some missiological
questions that challenge the churches regarding their stance on
solidarity with women.[5] The gathering in San Antonio was

5. See unpublished Section Reports from the World Conference on
Mission and Evangelism convened by the World Council of Churches in San
Antonio, Texas, 22 May–1 June 1989.

uniquely multifaceted. People came from across the continents and from very diverse Christian traditions. Two concerns in particular that emerged from the conference constitute critical openings to the coming context in which the church is being called to carry forth God's mission. These two concerns also challenge the churches to be in solidarity with women. They are participation and the Eucharist.[6]

At San Antonio, the stories of people in mission at the grass roots raised questions about the meaning of mission in Christ's way. The conference proceedings did not include the presentation of position papers or carefully crafted missiological exegeses. Although these sorts of reflection are significant, they should follow, not force, the reflection of those engaged in mission. Only after the stories is it appropriate to relate the issues they raise to accumulated theological tradition. This task has yet to be undertaken.

As the movement of the Holy Spirit is creating communion among women and men in new communities, communities from which the word of the gospel will go forth to bear fruit, the structures of what we call church are also challenged to be shaped by this participatory style. More specifically, if churches are to be in solidarity with women during the Ecumenical Decade, this participatory style must be integral to the churches' own self-understandings. The churches must discover ways of *being* more participatory. A first step is to acknowledge the cries of women who feel alienated from present structures and the cries of those who feel discriminated against as they attempt to stay within present structures. Until the energies of all church members, women and men, are brought into a dynamic and transforming communion, churches will not be able to respond to the urging of the Spirit to move out in mission more holistically. Without the concerted energies of all members, the

6. Ibid.

churches will not be able to move the whole creation toward fulfillment according to God's plan.

A second missiological focus of attention is the Eucharist. The World Conference on Mission and Evangelism that was held in Melbourne, Australia, in 1980 gave special significance to the Eucharist as bread for the missionary journey.[7] At San Antonio, this new understanding of the Eucharist was embodied; indeed, the entire experience was eucharistic. True, the Eucharist was celebrated each morning, according to different traditions, at the edge of the conference site before daily proceedings began. In this sense, the Eucharist was on the periphery and, as such, raised a serious missiological question: What does it mean for the celebration of the Eucharist to be on the periphery of a gathering of Christians? But another aspect of the eucharistic reality present at the gathering was experienced in worship and in Bible study. As we gathered around the Word of God, many of us left asking with the disciples of Emmaus, "Did not our hearts burn within us while he talked with us on the road?" (Luke 24:32).

This experience of eucharistic reality pervading all of life leads us to look again at the interrelatedness of all of life. It calls for our commitment to changing the course of the continuing destruction of God's creation. It calls for our commitment to uphold the integrity of creation, together with justice and peace. Response to this call can lead to costly discipleship. Yet, engaged in response to this call, peasants and bishops, women and men discover communion. A new martyrology, which preserves the names of sisters and brothers across six continents, bears witness to this discipleship, and their memory consecrates the consequent communion of the committed.

Communion—coming to be in new communities of witness, presence, solidarity, and participation—is a reality that

7. *Your Kingdom Come: Mission Perspectives* (Geneva: World Council of Churches, 1980), pp. 203-7.

reveals and expresses genuine discipleship today. This reality is arising from within the life of churches. This reality is a critical challenge if churches are to be in solidarity with women during the Ecumenical Decade and beyond. It is fundamentally a missiological challenge because it emerges in a particularly powerful way among those engaged in witness to the gospel in diverse ways. Solidarity, suffused with a burning desire for the promise of the kingdom to come, is the way many persons today experience God. This is grace for our time of transition.

Ecumenism and Feminism in Dialogue on Authority

Margaret O'Gara

WHAT can the ecumenical movement and the Christian feminist movement contribute to the discussion on authority in the church? What do they have to say to each other?

At first glance, ecumenists or feminists might answer, "Little or nothing." Some ecumenists see in the feminist movement—with its search for mutual recognition of ordained ministries and common structures of decision-making—only new obstacles in the path toward church unity. And some feminists see the movement for church unity as simply a confirmation of a patriarchal status quo, with new agreements reinforcing an old-boy network of episcopal and other ordained authorities.

Margaret O'Gara, a Roman Catholic, is Associate Professor of Theology in the University of St. Michael's College in Toronto. She is a member of the Anglican–Roman Catholic Dialogue of Canada, the Disciples of Christ–Roman Catholic International Commission for Dialogue, and the Catholic Network for Women's Equality. She is also past president of the North American Academy of Ecumenists.

To hear and take seriously the voices of both movements today is a demanding task.

But, as a member of both movements, I want to suggest that both ecumenism and feminism offer useful suggestions for the reform of the theology and practice of authority. In addition, each movement offers important criticisms of the other. By entering into dialogue with these movements and setting them in dialogue with each other, the churches that seek greater solidarity with women by the year 2000 will find themselves enriched.

Common Concerns of Ecumenism and Feminism on Authority

The two movements have a number of common concerns about authority. Each movement is actually very interested in authority and very critical of the way authority is often understood and practiced. This common concern about both the theoretical understanding of authority and the practice of authority in the life of the church helps make each of these movements a movement for reform and renewal of the church rather than simply a school of thought.

Feminism seeks to liberate the church from false interpretations of the Scriptures, interpretations supporting men's superiority or domination over women. "The Women's Movement errs when it dismisses the Bible as inconsequential or condemns it as enslaving," argues Phyllis Trible. "In rejecting Scripture women ironically accept male chauvinistic interpretations and thereby capitulate to the very view they are protesting." As she points out, "the hermeneutical challenge is to translate biblical faith without sexism."[1] To this end, Trible rereads the story of

1. Trible, "Depatriarchalizing in Biblical Interpretation," *Journal of the American Academy of Religion* 41 (1973): 31.

Adam and Eve to reveal their equality in creation; it is sin that
leads to a distortion of this good creation, that initiates a pattern
of domination and subjugation. To this end as well, Elisabeth
Schüssler Fiorenza criticizes the preachers and writers who
maintain "that the submission of women and their subordinate
place in family, society and church were ordained and revealed
in the Bible."[2] To counter this perspective, she points to the
non-sexist traditions that lie behind the New Testament, traditions of egalitarian and interpersonal styles of authority in early
Christian communities where both women and men exercised
ministries of leadership.[3] Other writers emphasize the positive
images of women in the Gospels,[4] or the favorable attitude of
Jesus toward women.[5]

At the same time, Schüssler Fiorenza echoes other writers
when she warns that the Bible itself contains an "androcentric
interpretation and selection of early Christian traditions." As
she explains, "*All* early Christian writings are culturally conditioned and formulated in a patriarchal milieu. Biblical revelation and truth are not found in a-cultural essence distilled from
patriarchal texts, but are given in those texts and interpretative
models which transcend and criticize their patriarchal culture

2. Schüssler Fiorenza, "The Study of Women in Early Christianity: Some
Methodological Considerations," in *Critical History and Biblical Faith: New
Testament Perspectives*, ed. Thomas J. Ryan (Villanova, Pa.: College Theology
Society, 1979), p. 35.

3. Ibid., pp. 41-45; cf. Elisabeth Schüssler Fiorenza, *In Memory of Her:
A Feminist Theological Reconstruction of Christian Origins* (New York:
Crossroad, 1983), pp. 97-241.

4. Raymond Brown, "Roles of Women in the Fourth Gospel," *Theological
Studies* 36 (1975): 688-99; cf. Constance Parvey, "The Theology and Leader-
ship of Women in the New Testament," in *Religion and Sexism: Images of Woman
in the Jewish and Christian Traditions*, ed. Rosemary Radford Ruether (New
York: Simon & Schuster, 1974), pp. 117-49; and Elisabeth Moltmann-Wendel,
The Women around Jesus (New York: Paulist Press, 1977).

5. Mary Rose d'Angelo, "Women and the Earliest Church: Reflecting on
the Problematique of Christ and Culture," in *Women Priests*, ed. Leonard
Swidler and Arlene Swidler (New York: Paulist Press, 1977), p. 195.

and religion."[6] Thus the authority of the Bible itself is rightly discerned only when it is read as living tradition, with a critical hermeneutic that seeks the liberating word of God's revelation in the midst of history.[7]

In addition to their commitment to eliminate false understandings of the authority of men over women in the Bible and even a false understanding of the authority of the Bible itself, feminists also wish to reread the Christian tradition in order to correct theology or practice that condones a pattern of men's domination over women in the church or the world. Margaret Farley looks for the sources of sexual inequality in the history of theology and finds them in "the identification of women with evil" and "the identification of the fullness of the *imago Dei* with male persons."[8] This identification was furthered by the probably unreflective appropriation of the cultural viewpoint during the patristic period, exemplified in Philo, which linked men with spirit and women with matter.[9] For centuries theologians used this faulty theological anthropology in a variety of forms to argue in favor of the subordinate character of women and against the ordination of women.[10] Feminist theologians are critical of ar-

6. Schüssler Fiorenza, "The Study of Women in Early Christianity," pp. 37, 39.

7. See Elisabeth Schüssler Fiorenza, "Feminist Spirituality, Christian Identity, and Catholic Vision," in *Womanspirit Rising: A Feminist Reader in Religion*, ed. Carol Christ and Judith Plaskow (San Francisco: Harper & Row, 1979), p. 146; and Elisabeth Schüssler Fiorenza, "Feminist Theology as a Critical Theology of Liberation," *Theological Studies* 36 (1975): 611-12, 616.

8. Farley, "Sources of Sexual Inequality in the History of Christian Thought," *Journal of Religion* 56 (1976): 164.

9. Rosemary Radford Ruether, "Misogynism and Virginal Feminism in the Fathers of the Church," in *Religion and Sexism*, ed. Rosemary Radford Ruether, pp. 150-83; cf. George Tavard, *Woman in Christian Tradition* (Notre Dame: University of Notre Dame Press, 1973), especially pp. 97-121.

10. Francine Cardman, "The Medieval Question of Women and Orders," *The Thomist* 42 (1978): 582-99.

guments based on such an unchristian anthropology, and they are ready to criticize contemporary uses of these traditions that would rest on such arguments—even the more subtle arguments of today which maintain that men and women are by nature complementary.[11] Similarly, they criticize presentations from Christian tradition that consistently portray God in male images or that use Christ's maleness as an argument against women's ordination. For them, such arguments and practices approach idolatry. As Mary Daly pointed out long ago, "If God is male, then the male is God."[12] This is a lesson about authority that feminists have learned well.

Feminists argue that because of women's experience of male domination and of marginalization in some decision-making roles, women are particularly sensitive to the misuse of authority. Such sensitivity alerts them to a host of abuses, ranging from the distorted use of authoritative sources to the dynamics of subjugating interpersonal relationships and the structures of power that can continue a patriarchal worldview or atmosphere. Accordingly, feminists urge the radical reform of the ordained ministry, not just its inclusion of women. Thus they also urge a model of consultation and consensus in decision-making, with an emphasis on the participation of all and on equality among members of the church. Many feminists seem wary of any authoritative traditions or leaders; they are quick to recognize the role of prophecy in the church, and they even describe the women's movement as a prophetic movement calling for repentance and reform of the church. For them, this is essential to being in Christ.

Ecumenism has a set of sensitivities and proposed reforms that are strikingly similar to those of feminism.

11. Margaret Farley, "Discrimination or Equality? The Old Order or the New?" in *Women Priests*, pp. 310-15; cf. Tavard, *Woman in Christian Tradition*, especially pp. 211-19.

12. Daly, *After the Death of God the Father*, 2nd ed. (Boston: Beacon Press, 1973), p. 19.

Ecumenists, too, know the dangers of a distorted use of the Scriptures as proof texts to illustrate the correctness of the views of the speaker or the speaker's tradition. The history of church divisions can be charted as a history of disagreements about the correct reading of the Scriptures. In order to be faithful to the authority of the Scriptures in their true meaning, groups involved in ecumenical dialogue consistently seek fresh readings of controversial scriptural texts,[13] sometimes appointing a special exegetical commission to study the scriptural questions before they begin their own work in the dialogue.[14]

At the same time, the ecumenical movement also stresses the importance of reading the Scriptures within a living tradition. It is by Tradition, with its many traditions, that the gospel is carried through the centuries, stated the Faith and Order Commission that met in Montreal in 1963.[15] The Anglican–Roman Catholic International Commission (ARCIC) understands the role of authoritative teaching within this context. "All generations and cultures must be helped to understand that the good news of salvation is also for them," it argues. "It is not enough for the Church simply to repeat the original apostolic words. It has also prophetically to translate them in order that the hearers in their situation may understand and respond to

13. See, for example, Anglican–Roman Catholic International Commission, "Ministry and Ordination," #8, #13; "Authority in the Church II," #2-9, in *The Final Report* (London: SPCK and Catholic Truth Society, 1982); [U.S.] Lutheran–Roman Catholic Dialogue, "Differing Attitudes toward Papal Primacy," #9-13; "Teaching Authority and Infallibility in the Church," #5-16; "Justification by Faith," #122-49, in *Building Unity,* ed. Joseph A. Burgess and Jeffrey Gros (New York: Paulist Press, 1989).

14. See, for example, *Peter in the New Testament: A Collaborative Assessment by Protestant and Roman Catholic Scholars,* ed. Raymond Brown et al. (Minneapolis: Augsburg Publishing House, 1973); and *Mary in the New Testament: A Collaborative Assessment by Protestant and Roman Catholic Scholars,* ed. Raymond Brown et al. (Philadelphia: Fortress Press, 1978).

15. Faith and Order Commission, "Scripture, Tradition and Traditions," in *Fourth World Conference on Faith and Order,* ed. P. C. Rodger and Lukas Vischer (New York: Association Press, 1964), pp. 50-61.

them. All such restatement must be consonant with the apostolic witness recorded in the Scriptures."[16] Prophetic translation, says ARCIC, means defending the gospel against error and formulating it in fresh ways for every culture and age. Sometimes formulations of the living tradition of the church become authoritative, "part of its permanent witness."[17] But this occurs only when the whole church accepts these formulations. "The assent of the faithful is the ultimate indication that the Church's authoritative decision in a matter of faith has been truly preserved from error by the Holy Spirit," explains ARCIC.[18] Concerns about consensus models of decision-making, the conciliar nature of the church, and the prophetic promptings of the Spirit receive a great deal of attention in ecumenical proposals about authoritative sources.

Like the feminist movement, the ecumenical movement also knows about abuse of authority, and it resolutely argues against any ecclesiology that furthers such abuse. It begins its discussion of authority by focusing on the authority of Christ. "The confession of Christ as Lord is the heart of the Christian faith. To him God has given all authority in heaven and on earth. As Lord of the Church he bestows the Holy Spirit to create a communion of men [sic] with God and with one another. . . . The Church is a community which consciously seeks to submit to Jesus Christ."[19] All of the members of the church, through common life in the body of Christ, are enabled "so to live that the authority of Christ will be mediated through them."[20] While recognizing the variety of gifts, the ecumenical movement starts its discussion about gifts and ministries with the authority of Christ and the granting of the Holy Spirit to all who are baptized. "God bestows upon all baptized persons the anointing and the promise of the Holy Spirit,

16. "Authority in the Church I," #15, in *The Final Report*.
17. "Authority in the Church II," #24.
18. Ibid., #25.
19. "Authority in the Church I," #1, #4.
20. Ibid., #3.

marks them with a seal and implants in their hearts the first installment of their inheritance as sons and daughters of God," says *Baptism, Eucharist, and Ministry* (BEM).[21] At the same time, "the Holy Spirit also gives to some individuals and communities special gifts for the benefit of the Church, which entitle them to speak and be heeded."[22] It is in this context that ecumenical statements locate ordained ministry, and in general the ecumenical movement is more positive about ordained ministry than feminism has been. The ordained ministers are not only representatives of the community but also "representatives of Jesus Christ to the community."[23] The church needs such persons to be publicly and continually responsible for pointing to the church's dependence on Christ and thus providing within "a multiplicity of gifts, a focus of its unity."[24] ARCIC believes that such a ministry "is not an extension of the common Christian priesthood but belongs to another realm of the gifts of the Spirit."[25]

At the same time, ecumenical groups do not issue naive statements about ministry by the ordained. "The authorities in the Church cannot adequately reflect Christ's authority because they are still subject to the limitations and sinfulness of human nature," comments ARCIC. "Awareness of this inadequacy is a continual summons to reform."[26] Churches that wish to overcome their differences regarding ordained ministry "need to work from the perspective of the calling of the whole people of God," comments BEM.[27] "The authority of the ordained ministry is not to be understood as the possession of the ordained person but as a gift for the continuing edification

21. World Council of Churches, "Baptism," #5, in *Baptism, Eucharist, and Ministry* (Geneva: World Council of Churches, 1982).
22. "Authority in the Church I," #5.
23. "Ministry," #11, in *Baptism, Eucharist, and Ministry.*
24. Ibid., #8.
25. "Ministry and Ordination," #13.
26. "Authority in the Church I," #37.
27. "Ministry," #6.

of the body in and for which the minister has been ordained," it continues.[28] And while recommending the recovery of the threefold ministry, including an episcopal ministry of oversight, BEM states clearly, "The three-fold pattern stands evidently in need of reform. . . . [It] raises questions for all the churches."[29]

The ecumenical movement shows its sensitivity to abuse of authority particularly when it discusses the possibility that all churches might come into full communion with the bishop of Rome, whose oversight could provide a Petrine ministry or universal primacy for the sake of the unity of the whole church in the gospel. The Lutherans in the U.S. Lutheran–Roman Catholic Dialogue are ready to acknowledge the possibility "that God may show again in the future that the papacy is his [sic] gracious gift to his [sic] people."[30] But the Lutherans also point out frankly that full communion with the papacy was broken in the sixteenth century because the papal teaching and practice were in such need of reform that they seemed to contradict the gospel. If the papacy undergoes sufficient reform to serve the gospel, "papal primacy will no longer be open to many traditional Lutheran objections."[31] Legitimate diversity, collegiality, and subsidiarity are a quick checklist of principles that signers of the Common Statement suggest as means to the "renewal of papal structures."[32] The "one thing necessary," explain the Lutheran partners, ". . . is that papal primacy be so structured and interpreted that it clearly serve the gospel and the unity of the church of Christ, and that its exercise of power not subvert Christian freedom."[33]

28. Ibid., #15.
29. Ibid., #24-25.
30. [U.S.] Lutheran–Roman Catholic Dialogue, "Differing Attitudes toward Papal Primacy: Common Statement," #28.
31. Ibid.
32. Ibid., #22-25.
33. Ibid., #28.

ARCIC pays similar attention to the abuse of authority by those with the ministry of oversight in the church. "Although primacy and conciliarity are complementary elements of *episcope* [oversight] it has often happened that one has been emphasized at the expense of the other, even to the point of serious imbalance," they comment, adding, "When churches have been separated from one another, this danger has been increased."[34] ARCIC makes the point more bluntly when writing about the authority of the bishop of Rome among the churches, explaining that it "does not imply submission to an authority which would stifle the distinctive features of the local churches. The purpose of this episcopal function of the bishop of Rome is to promote Christian fellowship in faithfulness to the teaching of the apostles." To this they append a frank comment: "Neither theory nor practice, however, has ever fully reflected these ideals."[35]

Nevertheless, they believe that a universal primacy is "part of God's design" for the church.[36] A universal primate could make a decisive judgment that becomes part of the church's permanent witness, although its reliability would be ultimately indicated by its reception in the church. A ministry by the universal primate could serve the gospel by "helping the churches to listen to one another, to grow in love and unity, and to strive together towards the fullness of Christian life and witness."[37] When it acted this way, ARCIC points out, a universal primacy would serve the local churches and their communion. A universal primate should not stifle freedom, legitimate diversity, or local traditions, ARCIC continues in its frank, understated manner. Further, it agrees that "Anglicans are entitled to assurance that acknowledgement of the universal primacy of the bishop of Rome would not involve the suppression

34. "Authority in the Church I," #22.
35. Ibid., #12.
36. "Authority in the Church II," #15.
37. "Authority in the Church I," #21.

of theological, liturgical and other traditions which they value or the imposition of wholly alien traditions."[38]

In short, the ecumenical discussions are both enthusiastic about ordered ministries in the church and realistically critical of the actual ways that ministers have abused and can abuse their authority. At the core of this enthusiastic and critical perspective stands an ecclesiology of communion.[39] The ecumenical movement recovers this ecclesiology of communion from the New Testament and the patristic writings, with their emphasis on the local churches that are in communion with each other while retaining appropriate diversity. Ecumenical dialogues consistently reject a pyramidal ecclesiology, which has a top-down understanding of authority and tends to treat the local churches as part of a large, undifferentiated group directed from the top. Such pyramidal conceptions of the church are a recent innovation in theology, ecumenists point out, that developed after the church became divided. By recovering the scriptural and patristic vision of the church as a communion of local churches, ecumenists hope to find the usable traditions that once allowed Christians to remain in full communion.

I have been arguing that feminism and ecumenism have much more in common than might be recognized on first inspection. Let me summarize my points. Both movements seek the reform of the church in its theology and its practice. Both want to correct misreadings of the Scriptures. Both read the history of the church with a critical recognition of abuses and with a positive eye for the recovery of more authentic traditions, a usable past. Both believe that the church must act as a living tradition, subject to Christ and leery of idolatrous theories and

38. "Authority in the Church II," #22.
39. "Introduction," #1-9, in *The Final Report;* Joint Commission for Theological Dialogue between the Roman Catholic Church and the Orthodox Church, "The Mystery of the Church and of the Eucharist in the Light of the Mystery of the Holy Trinity," *One in Christ* 19 (1983): 188-97.

practices. Both emphasize decision-making by consensus and conciliar consultation. Both are suspicious of traditions that do not listen to all of the voices in the discussion.

Having covered this shared ground, let me give an example of the mutual misunderstanding between feminists and ecumenists. Last winter, one of my students in a theology course was a woman from the United Church of Canada seeking commission as a diaconal minister. In the paper she wrote on the issue of episcopal oversight, she commented, "The power base of episcopate begins with the pope, rather than the people; it is a top-down theory of power and authority, not a bottom-up theory of empowerment that I am used to. . . . For me, it epitomizes patriarchy." In the same month that I read this paper, Barbara Harris was elected by her diocese to be a bishop in the Episcopal Church in the United States. Some of my Roman Catholic colleagues as well as some vocal Anglican leaders saw Harris's episcopal consecration as the end of serious work for the unity of the Anglican and the Roman Catholic communions.

But both my student and my colleagues seemed to be overlooking possibilities. My student had failed to hear from ecumenists that they too oppose a "top-down" ecclesiology and that the ecclesiology of communion offers an understanding of the church that would respect the distinctive traditions of her own communion. My colleagues had failed to hear from feminists that they too seek to defend and translate the gospel in new ways and that they see in the consecration of a woman bishop the public stand taken against a faulty anthropology but taken within the historic structures of a threefold ministry so urged by ecumenists. An appreciation of the elements that ecumenism and feminism share might make them powerful partners in the work of reform of the church.

What Feminism and Ecumenism Can Teach
Each Other about Authority

The partnership of feminism and ecumenism would be strengthened if these two movements would also start learning from each other. I have dwelt at length on what they have in common, but let me say something more briefly about what they ought to be teaching each other.

Ecumenism could reap the benefit of the feminist movement, which crosses denominational lines in a startling way and brings thousands of Christians together with a passionate intensity of purpose. While talks on ecumenism may draw only a handful of listeners and books on ecumenism may have trouble finding readers, talks and books about women in the church attract large audiences. My women students, who come from a variety of church traditions, feel a deep kinship with each other as they ponder the reality of their positions within different church communities. The commonality of women's experience of and within the church can be a deeper bond among Christian women than church denominations. The ecumenical movement, which knows well the phenomenon of defining a tradition as "the other, not us," should welcome this recognition of commonality. Furthermore, it should examine the ways in which the church's theory and practice treat women as "other."

But, more fundamentally, the ecumenical movement needs to ask itself why feminism creates a bond of such passionate intensity among women, a bond that crosses denominational lines so effectively. I believe this bond develops because, for feminists, the truth of the gospel itself seems threatened by any theology or practice that legitimates men's domination over women. An Anglican bishop, himself a feminist, put it this way: "Would I really want to be in full communion with a church that did not ordain women?" This question is hard for him to answer. Theological anthropologies that identify women with subordinate roles, understandings of ordination which demand that those ordained be male because Christ was a male, doctrines of God that continually present God in male imagery—all of these seem to feminists to distort the gospel message in a fundamental way. When they hear ecumenical statements repeat such views or urge patience in the face of them, feminists wonder about the price of unity. Many of them see the relationship between ecumenism and feminism as a choice between unity and truth. Conceiving it this way, they choose truth. Shouldn't the ecumenical movement welcome the spirit of commitment to the fresh translation of the gospel's truth that such a choice represents?

In addition, the feminist movement might succeed in teaching ecumenists to reconceive the ordained ministry more thoroughly. An ecclesiology of communion should allow ecumenism to renew and reinterpret ordained threefold ministry so as not to confuse it with hierarchy. But too often ecumenical discussions can slip into hierarchical-business-as-usual in their consideration and implementation of mutual recognition of ordained ministries and of a Petrine ministry in the church. Feminism holds the promise of a fresh interpretation of ordination and other ministries that would free them from cultural forms apt to communicate domination rather than service.

Finally, feminist theology has raised a very important question in its criticism of some theological anthropologies used as arguments against the ordination of women. Rather than simply explaining or defending their church practice, ecumenists from churches that do not ordain women should also be willing to re-examine the arguments their churches use against this practice and to criticize these arguments when they are faulty. "Openness to each other holds the possibility that the Spirit may well speak to one church through the insights of another," BEM stated,[40] and the ecumenical movement should not miss this opportunity for a serious discussion of the substantive issues involved. Further-

40. "Ministry," #54.

more, as the Canadian Roman Catholic bishops recognized in their response to ARCIC, to use the disagreement about the ordination of women as an excuse to stop ecumenical work would be to miss the gospel mandate regarding the work for unity. "To allow the question of the ordination of women to delay the efforts to achieve full communion would be to disregard the urgency of Christ's mandate for unity," they observed.[41]

At the same time, the ecumenical movement has a good deal it can teach the feminist movement. While both movements in their contemporary form emerged at the beginning of this century, the ecumenical movement shows more skill at self-criticism than its counterpart. We might consider the reasons for this self-critical skill. I suggest that the ecumenical movement has a better sense of the pervasiveness of sin and the Fall.

Now what do I mean by that? I mean that feminism too often projects evil onto others: men, patriarchy, the institutional church, the ordained ministry. It is not adequately reflective about its own failings and sins. Women also are complicit in the structures of sin as well as solidary in the inheritance of grace, but some romantic feminists easily overlook this. Feminists who argue that women's different and special nature will overcome authoritarianism, abstract rationalism, militarism, and the rape of the earth seem a bit naive about their own potential for evil. Such views are not limited to feminists; Mother Teresa is reported to have said that women would make better priests than men. "No man can even come close to the love and compassion a woman is capable of giving," she is reported to have said (though she later denied making this statement).[42]

Some feminists, of course, have recognized this failure among their colleagues. In commenting on "romantic goddess"

41. Canadian Conference of Catholic Bishops, "Response of the Canadian Conference of Catholic Bishops to the ARCIC-I *Final Report*," *Ecumenism*, Dec. 1987, p. 15.

42. "Women Would Be Better Priests: Mother Teresa," Associated Press report in the *Toronto Star*, 1 Apr. 1984.

and Wicca or witchcraft forms of feminism, Rosemary Radford Ruether in 1980 warned against stereotypical identification of men or male systems with evil so that women "can be the great innocents or victims of history."[43] Such stereotypes, she suggests, are not really conducive to valid self-knowledge and development for women because they are rooted in a false anthropology. "Women need to acknowledge that they have the same drives and temptations to sin as males have—not just sins of dependency but also the sins of dominance, of which they have been less guilty not for want of capacity, but for want of opportunity. . . . If we are really to effect change, we must take responsibility for the capacities for both good and evil in all people," she observes. The creation of a feminist spirituality calls for "greater modesty and greater maturity than those still deeply wounded by patriarchal religion have generally been able to muster," she concludes.[44] More recently, black women have reminded their white sisters that feminist theology is complicit with evil when it is used to the advantage of the privileged speakers rather than as a means for overcoming oppression throughout the whole community.[45] But why are such warnings

43. Ruether, "Goddesses and Witches: Liberation and Countercultural Feminism," *Christian Century* 98 (1980): 844; cf. Rosemary Radford Ruether, *Sexism and God-Talk* (Boston: Beacon Press, 1983), pp. 104-9.

44. Ruether, "Goddesses and Witches," pp. 845, 847.

45. Jacquelyn Grant, "Introduction to Womanist Theology," a course at New York Theological Seminary, New York, New York, Jan. 1989; cf. Jacquelyn Grant, "Womanist Theology: Black Women's Experience as a Source for Doing Theology with Special Reference to Christology," *Journal of the Interdenominational Theological Center* 13 (Fall 1985–Spring 1986): 195-212; P. Murray, "Black Theology and Feminist Theology: A Comparative View," in *Black Theology: A Documentary History*, ed. J. H. Cone and G. S. Wilmore (Maryknoll, N.Y.: Orbis Books, 1979), pp. 398-414; *This Bridge Called My Back: Writings by Radical Women of Color*, ed. Cherrie Moraga and Gloria Anzuldua (Watertown, Mass.: Persephone Press, 1981); and Rosemary Radford Ruether, "Third World Women's Double Oppression," *National Catholic Reporter*, 11 Feb. 1983, p. 20.

necessary among feminists, and why are they not heeded more widely?

The ecumenical movement is founded on the insight that the division of the church contradicts the will of Christ; the fault for this situation was shared by all parties to the division. If the division of the church is to be overcome, a conversion is necessary: "There can be no ecumenism worthy of the name without a change of heart," taught Vatican II in its *Decree on Ecumenism.*[46] With conversion comes a confession of guilt for past errors by all of the churches who are speaking, along with a spirit of repentance. The church continually needs to be reformed; ecumenists are clear on this point. While such recognition does not seem to dampen their zeal for mutual criticism, perhaps it does make them more alert to the deep faults of their own traditions and more ready to hear good from those with whom they disagree. Even the incredibly painstaking process of writing by consensus demanded by agreed-upon statements of ecumenical-dialogue groups—when every participant must agree to every word—calls for a high degree of receptivity and repentance. Feminists warn often against idolatrous ideas, and correctly; but ecumenists know perhaps more deeply how easily we can make our own communities and convictions into idols. By giving a central place to repentance and conversion from the evil in which all of the participants are complicit, the ecumenical movement is more prepared to be self-critical and to grow.

The sense of sin is especially important in the attitude toward tradition and its reform, a significant and delicate matter for both feminists and ecumenists. The proper response to tradition, Georges De Schrijver suggests, demands both appreciative understanding of a tradition and a stance of suspicion or critical distance from which one asks questions like these: Why should

46. *Decree on Ecumenism [Unitatis redintegratio]*, #7, in *The Documents of Vatican II*, ed. Walter M. Abbot, S.J. (New York: Guild Press, 1966).

I listen to this tradition? Who was excluded from its formulation?[47] But we could add that if both understanding and critical query are necessary, the first must precede the second. Criticisms based on a misunderstanding of a tradition are not ultimately very helpful, even when they seek to serve a good aim.

Ecumenists have learned well the need to understand traditions sympathetically before criticizing them. In fact, one could understand the whole of the ecumenical movement as a commitment to the first moment of a response to tradition— the sympathetic grasp of a tradition, especially a tradition not one's own. Ecumenism is fueled by the conviction that Christians are in real if not full communion and by the suspicion that many ideas once thought contradictory may turn out to be compatible if more deeply explored. Training in the ecumenical dialogue schools participants to give the benefit of the doubt to the partner first and only then to ask, in the spirit of the gospel, about understandings or practices that seem wrong or unfaithful.

Feminists might benefit from such training. Two areas come specifically to mind.

Feminists should be more discriminating in their criticisms of the past if they have not really grasped what earlier thinkers were saying. Eliminating the doctrine of the Trinity without a hearing would seem a serious mistake for Christian feminists to risk, but I do not hear them expressing much concern about this. The issue of baptism provides another example. At last the churches have begun to recognize each other's baptism, after working toward this goal for decades. What some feminists propose to do about baptism—blithely to eliminate the baptismal formula used for centuries of the church's history and to replace it with formulations made up in the last ten years— seems to overlook the complexity of the issues involved. Other

47. De Schrijver, "Hermeneutics and Tradition," *Journal of Ecumenical Studies* 19 (1982): 32-47.

possible omissions of things both established and valuable come to mind. The role of repetition in worship, the significance of biblical language, the value of a shared formulation, the language of mutuality and egalitarian relationship implied in Trinitarian "person" talk—all of this can be overlooked in some feminist proposals of the Creator-Redeemer-Sanctifier type. Such forgetfulness would be unfortunate.

By making these comments I am not equating a change of baptismal formula with the elimination of the doctrine of the Trinity. But helpful proposals have been made for the recovery of earlier baptismal formulations and even for the introduction of new Trinitarian language, proposals that are neither patriarchal nor naively innovative and that show more understanding of the depth of the Trinitarian issues involved.[48] Feminists would draw more authentically on their own respect for consensus if they attended more carefully to such a widespread foundational tradition about God as a communion of mutual love.

Another issue pertaining to tradition and its reform is the issue of ordained ministry and other structures of authority in the church. As I said before, feminist theology gives the church a good opportunity to rethink the nature of the ordained ministry and the relationship of ordained ministers to the whole community. On the other hand, feminists might show a more realistic appreciation for structures, however flawed, that have served the proclamation of the gospel and the unity of the church. This caveat might be extended to our discussion of

48. David R. Holeton, "Changing the Baptismal Formula: Feminist Proposals and Liturgical Implications," *Ecumenical Trends* 17 (1988): 69-72; cf. Catherine Mowry LaCugna, "Baptism, Feminists, and Trinitarian Theology," *Ecumenical Trends* 17 (1988): 65-68. For insightful discussions showing the positive value of new proposed formulations or images, see Mary Rose D'Angelo, "Beyond Father and Son," in *Justice as Mission: An Agenda for the Church*, ed. Terry Brown and Christopher Lind (Burlington, Ont.: Trinity Press, 1985), pp. 107-18; and Elizabeth A. Johnson, "The Incomprehensibility of God and the Image of God Male and Female," *Theological Studies* 45 (1984): 462-63.

ministries of oversight in the church. The Canadian Roman Catholic bishops have warned against a utopian attitude, commenting, "Reconciliation of our communions ought not to be delayed by false hopes for a utopian ideal."[49] While we should not use such an insight as an excuse to avoid the difficult work of reforming the church, should it not at least be a part of our dialogue?

Conclusion

I have been arguing that the ecumenical movement and the feminist movement have a great deal in common. In addition, I have urged them to learn something from each other.

It is not hard for the churches to be in solidarity with women over the next decade. What is hard is the reform of the exercise of authority in the church for the sake of the mission of the gospel. Both ecumenism and feminism are movements for reform in the church. Each has something to teach and something to learn if its contributions are to be used to best advantage. That may take us more than a decade, but we could begin the work that needs to be done.

49. "Response of the Canadian Conference of Catholic Bishops to the ARCIC-I *Final Report*," pp. 16-17.

III TOWARD A NEW ECUMENICAL MOVEMENT

Toward a New Ecumenical Movement: A Malawian Perspective

Annie Machisale-Musopole

IN 1988 I attended two ecumenical conferences held at Château de Bossey near Geneva. The themes of these conferences were "Reading the Bible with Women's Eyes" and "Confessing Jesus Christ in Africa Today." I contributed to these conferences by speaking about the differences between women's status in African religions and women's status in Christianity. African religion in the context of the Chewa culture, which is my native culture, values women as the source of the life of the community. Women are also valued as the source of communication between God and human beings, since God spoke to the Chewa people through women. In contrast, Christianity does not regard women with respect. This lack of respect is all the more striking because in Christianity women are the carriers of the faith from generation to generation, just as women are

Annie Machisale-Musopole is an active lay member of the Church of Central Africa–Presbyterian who leads Bible studies in American churches and has traveled in Europe and Africa on speaking tours focusing on women's issues. At present she is studying secretarial sciences in New York City.

the carriers of belief for the Chewa people. Accordingly, Christian churches are challenged not only to preach but also to live the liberating gospel. The ecumenical movement is also challenged, because rather than being the vanguard it has stepped to the sidelines to be a spectator as women struggle to give birth to a new creation. I will share my people's story to concretize the challenges confronting churches and councils during the Ecumenical Decade of Churches in Solidarity with Women.

Women's Status in Chewa Religion

As I have mentioned, women are accorded respect by Chewa religion. They are seen to be the source of the community's life and the source of communication with God, ancestors, and nature. They are perceived as the source of life because both male and female children come into the world through women's wombs. The art of creating and sustaining life is understood to be a secret between God and women. Women are considered to be co-creators with God.

In addition, the Chewa culture is matriarchal, and women are prophetic figures. In early times a woman named Makewana was a prophet who led all the people in the worship of God. Makewana means "the mother of all the children"; Makewana's official name, Chauta, means "God's representative." Makewana had young girls as her priests or assistants. These young girls were called *Matsanno,* meaning "graves," because they represented the ancestral spirits. In these times women talked directly to God. The people believed that God understood the language of women because God gave women what they prayed for.

Makewana was a leader as well as a prophetic figure in her community. She adjudicated disputes and gave orders to men and women alike. When Makewana died, her successor was chosen by spiritual revelation. These women were the pillars of the church in Chewa culture.

Women were also important in Chewa culture because they had status as rainmakers. Augustine Musopole explains:

> As to the origin of the Chewa, we have three traditions. The first one claims that the Chewa came from the Great Lakes area of East Africa led by a female rain caller by the name of Mangadzi and her Chembe. This group was also known by the name of a Wanda or Kalimanjira and [is] said to have settled along the lake shore in Tongaland. These are the people we have referred to as the proto-Chewa. Wherever they settled, they organized them-selves into chiefdoms under leading families and were ruled by famous rainmakers.[1]

These women rainmakers were consulted and led the commu-nity in prayer for rain when there was a drought. The rainmakers would order the people to perform various rituals while they prepared for worship. For example, a rainmaker sometimes ordered the community to abstain from sexual activities for several days, after which she would summon the people to worship at the shrine *Kachisi*. The rainmaker might pray like this: "*Naphriri*, we your children have come with broken hearts. We know that we have sinned before God. We beg you to apologize on our behalf to our mother God. Ask her to forgive sins we committed these past days." And the people replied, "Sorry! Sorry! Sorry! S-o-r-r-y!"

The worshippers would bring sacrifices to the shrine— goats, doves, chickens, flour, beer. If the worship centered on a plea for rain, then black goats, chickens, and doves were sacri-ficed. If the worship centered on confession, then white goats, chickens, and doves were sacrificed. The rainmaker always wore a black cloth. She never cut her hair, for to do so would shut out the rain. A shorn head symbolized a rainless sky.

---

1. Musopole, "The Chewa Concept of God and Its Implications for the Christian Faith," M.A. thesis, Chancellor College, University of Malawi, 1984, p. 21.

Christianity Meets African Religion: A World Destroyed

I asked my mother, "Why did the white missionary tell us that man was created first? Why did the white missionary tell us the God we should worship is the God of Abraham, Isaac, and Jacob?" My mother replied, "The white missionary was jealous of our ancestors, because when we pray the God of our ancestors hears us. The white missionaries want to destroy us and our culture."

When I studied history in my Malawian high school, I discovered that the white Christian missionaries who came to Africa to preach the gospel of justice and peace brought injustice and unrest instead. They destroyed the world that God created outside the Western world which they knew and controlled. Under the canopy of Christianity, the white missionaries colonized our culture. They imposed a government that was headed by a white man. They brought an army with guns.

And that was not all. Missionaries came with churches called denominations, creating divisions that destroyed the unity of God's creation. Protestants denounced Catholics. Catholics denounced Protestants. Each church or denomination claimed to be the true church. Anyone converted by a denomination different from one's own was an enemy.

Furthermore, missionaries imposed alien concepts on the Chewa people — for example, the worship of a God with foreign names and ancestors they did not know. Prophet Makewana had led the Chewa people in worship to a God who was known to them by the symbol of a woman. The names for God were names the Chewa people knew: "Chauta," Mother of all Children; "Chanjili," the Judge; "Mphambe," Undying God; "Kadzilenge," the One who is self-created and who created many others. White missionaries thought that the Chewa and other African peoples were worshipping idols because our God had names not unlike those of the hens in Mr. Brown's henhouse back home. The missionaries did not understand that these

were names for one God and that particular names were used
for particular purposes in worship. Because they did not or
would not understand, the missionaries destroyed the relationship of the Chewa people with God, the ancestors, nature, and
each other.

At the hands of the missionaries, African women became
slaves in their own countries. The missionaries taught that
women who were prophets were demons who would burn in
hell. Women were called to repent, and they were rendered
useless. The missionaries also told African men that women
could not be dominant figures in the household. Then the
missionaries placed African men in charge of their women and
children, while *they* were in charge of the African men and their
families. In other words, African men had their property, wives,
and children, and the white missionaries had their property and
African men and their families.

But African men were themselves caught in a vicious circle
of enslavement. They did forced labor. If they were paid at all,
it was only a few pennies. The women brewed beer and raised
the money to pay taxes for their men and themselves. In church
they were taught things counter to their experience. Men were
told that Adam was created first and that woman is a helper (a
slave) of man, who is her master. Moreover, African men were
taught that white men are superior because they have white
skin and because their greater intelligence is a sign that they
are nearer to God.

So women were to submit to men and African men and
women were to submit to their white masters. If a master beat
them, they should turn the other cheek. Christianity was not a
message of justice or peace or love. Christianity made African
women hate their masters—their husbands and white men—
and it pitted men against their brothers.

An added source of suffering for my people was the so-
called civilization that was introduced under the canopy of
Western Christianity. Two of its darker consequences were the

Arab slave trade and the Ngoni wars. The Arabs captured
people from villages in Malawi and all over Africa and then
sold them at the Port of Mombassa in East Africa to European
and American merchants. Some of the people were brought to
the Americas to work on the sugar plantations. The Ngoni wars
were brought to Malawi by the white people who came to South
Africa. These people came under the pretense of preaching
Christianity, but then they discovered gold and the other min-
eral wealth of the country. They fought and killed Chaka Zulu,
the paramount chief of the Zulu people. The Zulus, also known
as Ngonis, consequently came to Central and East Africa in
search of food and suitable land, waging wars of conquest to
get what they needed. In these and other ways European
colonialism destroyed life as a whole in the world of my people.

Women's Leadership in Malawian Society

This story of a foremother of mine is a resource for redeeming
such destruction. My great-grandmother, Anna Naphiri, told
me that her mother was a great military leader. My great-grandmother, for whom I was named, told me that her village suffered
attacks by the Ngoni warriors, who continually killed villagers
and stole their food and animals. The Ngoni would even time
their assaults, attacking after the harvest had been gathered,
and the villagers became familiar with this pattern. My great-
great-grandmother decided to do something about this. After
the harvest one year, she told all the men to go underground
to hide. She then organized the women of the village. They
were to arm themselves with spears and axes; some of them
were to beat drums to announce the Ngoni attackers. When
the Ngoni war cry could be heard, these women responded with
their own war cry. "Eh! Eh! Wanya!" they cried, meaning
"Watch out! Watch out! You are dead!" When the Ngoni warriors saw women with spears jumping and stabbing the ground,

they ran away. Then the men of the village came out of hiding and pursued the Ngoni. After this incident, the village of my great-great-grandmother was not attacked again.

The leader of the Malawi, Dr. H. Kamuzu Banda, understands and honors women's heritage of leadership in their communities. Dr. Banda, who broke the colonial yoke from the necks of Malawian men and women, has encouraged women to be educated, to be trained, to work hand-in-hand with men in civil service and in the private sector. Women and men are paid the same salary for the same work and are able to enjoy the same privileges. Women are also members of parliament in the Malawi Congress Party. They have served as chairpersons and cabinet ministers.

In Chewa cultural tradition, there is a royal lineage that follows the hierarchy of seniority. It does not matter if the person next in line of succession to leadership is a woman. Whenever a position is vacated, a woman can be appointed by the president or chosen by the people. Women have been chosen as chiefs and as such have had considerable authority. In fact, throughout the country there are many women chiefs—called Traditional Authorities—who sit on thrones and rule various regions. Among them are Chief Khongoni and Chief Kalolo of the Lilongwe District and Chief Kuluunda of the Salima District.

A Challenge to the Church in Malawi

The Church of Central Africa–Presbyterian became independent from its mother church in Scotland in 1958, before the country of Malawi was independent. But, unlike the Malawi government, which supports women and advocates women's achievements, the church discourages women. It is telling that the church did not change its rules regarding the role of women after it became independent. The church still argues that

women's proper place is not in ordained ministry. Although the
mother church in Scotland now ordains women, women in the
Church of Central Africa–Presbyterian are, tragically, still
trapped in the colonial caste system.

A question haunts me as I hear the passages that are said
to ordain women's subordination to men, passages such as Ephe-
sians 5:21-32 and 1 Timothy 2:8-15: How can God, who dwelt
in the womb of a woman, be a man's God? Mary is the mother
of Jesus. How can the Church of Central Africa–Presbyterian,
part of the wider church of Jesus Christ, be for men only?

I am strengthened in my faith and for the struggle as I recall
the words of the angel to Mary:

> "Hail, O favored one, the Lord is with you!" . . . "Do not be
> afraid, Mary, for you have found favor with God. And behold,
> you will conceive in your womb and bear a son, and you shall
> call his name Jesus." (Luke 1:28, 30-31)

Some men preach that women, not men, sinned and still cause
men to sin. But God showed favor to a woman for the sake of
redeeming both women and men. Through Mary, God entered
into a new covenant with humanity. When Mary said, "Behold,
I am the handmaid of the Lord" (Luke 1:38), she became the
new Eve. The old Eve has passed away. God has honored
women, making them mothers of God, mothers of a new creation.

In fact, despite the disproportionate official power wielded
by men in the Church of Central Africa–Presbyterian, women
are the church's backbone. They hold the revival meetings,
converting people and forming them in the faith. The women's
group—called Mvano in Blantyre Synod, Chigwilizano in
Nkhoma Synod, and Umanyano in Livingstonia Synod—
teaches Sunday school and adult-education courses, visits the
sick, and carries out other charitable acts. A proverb, passed
on to me by Mercy Amba Oduyoye, describes the situation

perfectly: "The hen knows when it is daylight, but it leaves it to the cock to make an announcement." The men make the announcements in church, and the male pastor preaches to the people whom the women have brought into the church.

The name of one of the women's groups, Mvano, is significant, as Dr. Silas C. Mcozana explains:

> The name Mvano means "mutual agreement." It implies cooperating in achieving a set goal, or working and living together in fellowship. . . . The name Mvano signifies a togetherness in Christ which is rooted in the Gospel and which extends beyond the church walls into the world. In bearing the name Mvano, Christian women stand out as servants of Christ among all women inside and outside the church.[2]

Having lifted up this model of mutuality, Dr. Mcozana goes on to say this:

> In 1971, the Presbyterian Church in Malawi trained its first female theological student. However, this student was never ordained. She now works with the Mvano and has made a significant contribution towards raising the ambitions of Mvano members to study theology. Other young women have followed her example, but no one has yet been ordained. What happens concerning the ordination of women in the remaining four years of the eighties depends on the women themselves, and on how much pressure they will be able to exert on the church to make it change its rigid law against women's ordination.[3]

This last comment disappoints me. Dr. Mcozana, like most other men, leaves women to our own struggle. Because of what he said about women as models of mutuality, his comment is even harder to take—it is not at all in the spirit of the Ecumenical

---

2. Mcozana, "Mvano and Evangelism in the Synod of Blantyre," *African Theological Journal* 3 (1986): 187.

3. Ibid.

Decade. The decade is not a challenge to women to continue to put pressure on the churches. It is a challenge to the churches to be in solidarity with women for the sake of community.

The gospel of Jesus Christ calls the churches in Malawi and around the world to change the status of women. God did not put man in charge of woman. God created male and female in God's own image. Women were given authority by God in Jesus Christ. This authority is akin to the authority accorded women by Chewa culture. Makewana led the community in worship, and God heard the prayers of the people. Why is it that women cannot lead worship in Malawian churches today? The church in Malawi may not be the bearer of hope for women, since the women in that church are caught in a colonial caste system. Wherever that hope may come from, we are calling for renewal, and we are calling for it to begin soon.

A Challenge toward a New Ecumenical Movement

In Malawi we live in communities called villages, where people live for one another. We are community-oriented people. When a child of the community achieves an honor, it is a joy for all of us. When a problem plagues one family, it is a problem for all of us. There is a saying in the Tumbuka language, "Kawepano nkhatonse," which means "What falls here is for us all." A saying in the Chewa language, "Nsomba ikawola imodzi zawola zonse," has a similar meaning: "When one fish in a sack is rotten, all the fish in the sack are deemed rotten because the whole sack stinks."

The ecumenical movement is a global village. Accordingly, its aims should be to bring together the people belonging to different faiths and different Christian traditions. The ecumenical movement is a call to cooperate to accomplish the goals of our global village. It is a call to devote ourselves to one another as to Christ. But the ecumenical movement will die if it is marred by new divisions as we seek to overcome old divisions. From my experience in ecumenical gatherings, I am aware of racial, regional, national, and gender discrimination. As I see it, the ecumenical movement does not embody its confession of concern for all God's people. We must work to change this, to make the ecumenical movement what it is meant to be. The ecumenical movement is called to be a lamp shining to show that in Jesus Christ there is neither male nor female, neither poor nor rich, neither black nor white. The ecumenical movement is called to be a global village wherein all God's people live with and for one another. "What falls here is for us all."

A New Phase in the Ecumenical Movement: One Woman's Perspective on Asian Activities

Sun Ai Lee Park

THE new phase in the ecumenical movement is signaled in the women's movement and in the movements of various peoples. In this essay what I want to do primarily is not make a prediction for the future but seek the significance of current phenomena in relation to the ecumenical movement in Asia. I will focus my reflections on activities in Korea and Japan as well as on the Christian Conference of Asia. By focusing on these particular signs of a new phase, I hope to illumine a new phase for the ecumenical movement worldwide.

Before I discuss these signs of a new phase, I will reflect a bit on the past from the perspective of W. A. Visser 't Hooft, focusing particularly on his book entitled *Has the Ecumenical Movement a Future?*[1]

1. Visser 't Hooft, *Has the Ecumenical Movement a Future?* (Belfast, Ireland: Christian Journals Ltd., 1974).

Sun Ai Lee Park, an ordained minister of the Christian Church (Disciples of Christ), is editor of In God's Image, *the monthly journal published by the Asian Women's Resource Centre for Culture and Theology. She is also the editor, together with Virginia Fabella, M.M., of* We Dare to Dream: Doing Theology as Asian Women.

Happenings in the Past

The ecumenical movement emerged out of the nineteenth-century missionary movement when churches confessed the scandal of their divisions on the mission fields. Accordingly, W. A. Visser 't Hooft marks the beginning of the ecumenical movement as coincident with the 1910 World Missionary Conference. The energy generated by this conference for evangelization, enunciated most powerfully by John R. Mott, gave rise to the International Missionary Council, the first of several developments that would eventually come together to form the World Council of Churches. The seeds of the second of these three developments were also sown at the 1910 conference. Charles Brent, Anglican bishop of the Philippines, saw that the next step on the road to unity was to work for agreement on matters of faith and order. The third development, the Life and Work movement, was spearheaded by Swedish bishop Nathan Soderblom as a call to the churches to respond together to urgent issues of the day without waiting for doctrinal agreement.

According to Visser 't Hooft's account, the second phase of the ecumenical movement began in 1934 when it confronted the church struggle in Germany. That year the central question before the Life and Work conference in Fanø, Denmark, was whether to take sides with the Confessing Churches or to remain neutral. Visser 't Hooft recalled, "George Bell, Bishop of Chichester, who had kept himself closely informed by Dietrich Bonhoeffer, realized that the Confessing Church was defending central Christian Principles, on the validity of which depended the existence of the whole ecumenical movement. In the end, the meeting expressed itself both in word and in deed for the encouragement of the Confessing Church."[2] Four years later, at the second world conference of Life and Work, participants recognized that they needed more than a sociological perspective on the church if the church was to witness in the face of

2. Ibid., p. 16.

current world problems. From this conference came renewed conviction that there is a communion with a firmer foundation. In Visser 't Hooft's words, "The threat of war and the war itself gave the ecumenical movement the great opportunity to prove that the movement towards unity by Christians was not just a by-product of a worldly internationalism, but drew its strength from the very essence of the church."[3]

The third phase of the ecumenical movement was initiated when the World Council of Churches was officially instituted in 1948. Although the cold war was dividing people into camps, this was a time of both consolidation and expansion for the ecumenical movement. The Christian churches were mobilized for spiritual and material reconstruction after the war. These tasks signaled not only solidarity among all Christians but also their solidarity with all who suffer. Also, even though the cold war between East and West predominated during this phase, some attention was paid to Third World peoples and churches.

The fourth phase, a time of flowering and harvesting, began in the 1960s. At this point the International Missionary Council was incorporated into the World Council. The Russian Orthodox Church, along with a number of other Orthodox churches, became members of the council. Conversation developed between the World Council of Churches and the Roman Catholic Church when Pope John XXIII established the Vatican Secretariat for Promoting Christian Unity. Regional councils such as the East Asia Christian Council also began to emerge.

During these years it became clear that different peoples and churches have quite different priorities. This recognition of diversity is still challenging the ecumenical movement. Among other things, integrally involving the peoples and churches of color in what began as a white Western ecumenical movement remains a profound challenge at the present time.

3. Ibid., p. 18.

A New Phase in the Ecumenical Movement

The new phase in the ecumenical movement is marked by two great movements: the women's movement and the movement of various peoples in grass-roots contexts. Just as the ecumenical movement was initiated by white Western men, so the women's movement was initiated by white Western women. Already in the late eighteenth century and the nineteenth century, women in Europe struggled to attain various legal rights, including rights to property and education. The right to vote was predominant, a right that was finally won by British women in 1915 and by American women in 1920. In the 1960s, a second wave of the women's movement swelled as women began to recognize patriarchy's pervasive power to oppress women. Feminist theology, also initiated by white Western women, was a response to patriarchal theology and the patriarchal church.

The years 1974 and 1975 were marked by two conferences that broadened and deepened awareness of the lives of Third World women. The first conference was organized by the World Council of Churches' Sub-Unit on Women in Church and Society; held in West Berlin, the conference was titled "Sexism in the 1970s: Discrimination against Women." The second conference was the World Conference of the International Women's Year, sponsored by the United Nations and held in Mexico City. Women from all over the world participated in these two conferences. Although one conference was Christian and the other was secular, what they had fundamentally in common was the voices of Third World women. These women spoke about the sexism in their own societies but made it clear that combatting sexism alone would not solve their problems. From the perspective and experience of these women, sexism must be linked with racism and with colonial or neo-colonial economic and political domination. Combatting sexism alone is the privilege of white, middle-class Western women. Solidarity among women around the world cannot be forged solely on

the basis of sexism. Women's liberation must be set within the
context of the struggle for human liberation.

The United Nations Decade for Women, the proposal for
which came from the Mexico City conference, helped forge
solidarity among women worldwide. This solidarity was signaled
at the end of the decade at the U.N.–sponsored NGO Forum
'85 held in Nairobi. Approximately 14,000 women from around
the world gathered in Nairobi for the forum. Matsui Yayori, a
Japanese journalist who attended both the U.N.–sponsored
events, offered these comments:

> In the developed nations of the North, where the women's lib-
> eration movement has been rooted to some degree, there has
> been an expansion of interest in the conditions of women in the
> Third World. Betty Friedan, the tough-line leader of the Ameri-
> can women's group to Mexico, had taken the line of pluralism in
> Nairobi. This made evident the fact that women have come to
> recognise the theories of the liberation movement according to
> the realities of their own region. Charlotte Bunch, an American
> member of the Steering Committee of the Forum, expressed her
> solidarity with the women of the Third World as follows: "We
> need the global perceptions of the reality that our country is in
> control of the daily life of women in developing countries."[4]

Western Christian women are called to echo their secular sisters. We need to listen to Christian women in the Third World
as we identify issues most pressing for us, including women's
ordination and the development of theology from the perspective of our own contexts.

The Ecumenical Association of Third World Theologians,
EATWOT, has provided another forum in which Third World
women can speak. In 1981, EATWOT established a Women's
Commission in response to the voices of women. Virginia Fabella
and Mercy Amba Oduyoye comment on this development:

4. Yayori, "In Solidarity with Women of the World: Embarkation Towards
the Year 2000," *In God's Image*, Oct. 1985, p. 10.

Sexism . . . existed with[in] the Association itself. Our voices were not being heard, although we were visible enough. It became clear to us that only the oppressed can truly name their oppression. We demanded to be heard. The result was the creation within EATWOT of a Women's Commission, and not a Commission on Women as some of the male members would have it. Rather than see ourselves solely as victims of male domination, we formed a sisterhood of resistance to all forms of oppression, seeking creative partnership with men of the Association.[5]

In December 1986, Third World women gathered for the first time in Oaxtepec, Mexico, to reflect on what it means to do theology from their perspectives. Preparation for the conference had taken place in national consultations and in sub-continental and continental consultations. With each phase of this process there had been renewed commitment to the belief "that no experience was too marginal to be included in the global."[6]

There are other ecumenical organizations that engage women doing theology. Among these are the Christian Conference of Asia and the World Student Christian Federation, whose Asia and Pacific regional office in Hong Kong has a Women's Commission. The Association for Theological Education in Southeast Asia and the Program for Theology and Culture in Asia are also attempting to engage Asian women theologians in their conferences.

The Asian Women's Resource Centre for Culture and Theology in Hong Kong, established in 1988, is taking the lead in strengthening and supporting Asian women theologians. First and foremost, the center organizes the theological consultations and programs of Asian women. Another key activity of the center is the publication of In God's Image, the

5. With Passion and Compassion: Third World Women Doing Theology, ed. Virginia Fabella, M.M., and Mercy Amba Oduyoye (Maryknoll, N.Y.: Orbis Books, 1988), p. x.
6. Ibid.

quarterly journal begun in 1982 and published with the help
of the Christian Conference of Asia as "an Asian Christian
women's effort to provide a forum for expressing our reality,
our struggles, our faith reflections and our aspirations for
change." (When the Christian Conference of Asia was forced
out of Singapore, production of the journal was moved to the
Asian Women's Resource Centre in Hong Kong.) The center
has also published two books. The first is the report of the
Consultation on Asian Women's Theology held in Singapore
in 1987. The second book is a collection of the theological
writings of Asian women entitled *We Dare to Dream: Doing
Theology as Asian Women*.[7]

The Movement of Peoples in Asia

This movement of peoples occurs most often outside traditional
theological definitions of God's people. In his keynote address
to the Asian Mission Consultation held in Cipanas, Indonesia,
Dr. Kim Yong-Bock challenged Asian Christians' definition of
God's people, a definition that tends to be narrowed by our
minority status in the populations of Asia. Yong-Bock said, "The
most basic theological affirmation is that the peoples of Asia
are the children of God. God the Creator is the God of the
suffering and struggling peoples of Asia, no matter who they
are in terms of religion, political ideology, or cultural differences." This affirmation is a challenge to us Asian Christians.
What Yong-Bock is saying is that our minority status as Asian
Christians must also be the basis for our striving to be in solidarity with all God's struggling and suffering people. The challenge
for Asian Christians in the ecumenical movement is to join

7. *We Dare to Dream: Doing Theology as Asian Women*, ed. Virginia Fabella,
M.M., and Sun Ai Lee Park (Hong Kong: Asian Women's Resource Centre
for Culture and Theology, 1989).

hands with these people to work on the problems of poverty, prostitution, migrant labor, ecological destruction, and nuclear exposure, work that needs to be undertaken for the sake of the whole creation.

One example of this movement of peoples comes from Japan. In August 1989, sixteen grass-roots conferences were organized by the Asia Pacific Resource Centre based in Tokyo, Japan. At these conferences, a variety of issues were discussed, including farmers and food, the plight of indigenous peoples, education, human rights, women's status, militarism, ecological crisis, and development. All delegates to these conferences finally gathered in Minamata, a fishing village badly victimized by industrial pollution. There the delegates issued a declaration that begins with this statement:

> As it did to the people of Bhopal and Chernobyl, a giant organization with advanced science, technology and production techniques condemned the people of Minamata to fear, sickness and death, and their beautiful bay to irreparable damage. These three disasters—Minamata, Bhopal, and Chernobyl—can be taken as benchmarks of our time. At Minamata, the industry of a capitalist country poisoned its own citizens. At Bhopal, a U.S. multinational corporation poisoned people of the South. At Chernobyl, a socialist government spilled radiation out over its land and people, and beyond its borders to the whole world.[8]

The declaration goes on to address the land rights of indigenous peoples in the face of the confiscation and exploitation of their land by large industries that have government endorsement. As more and more agribusiness comes to Asia, the very survival of indigenous people as well as of their land is at stake. The third article of the declaration, an article on women, deserves to be quoted in full:

8. See "An Alliance of Hope: The Minamata Declaration," 24 Aug. 1989, Minamata, Japan.

For women, development has meant disempowerment of all kinds. They have been marginalized and subordinated by male religions, male science and knowledge, and male maldevelopment. The billion-dollar pornography and sex industry has reduced them to mere commodities. At the same time, they continue to be subordinated within their own homes.

The Minamata gathering and its declaration are signs of the solidarity emerging from the movement of peoples in Asia.

The Spirituality of the Movement of Women and the Movement of the Peoples of Asia

At the meeting of the WCC's Commission on Faith and Order in Budapest, Hungary, in August 1989, I had a conversation with Emilio Castro, the council's general secretary. I asked him what he thinks the new phase of the ecumenical movement is or will be. He replied, "Now we need to search for the spirituality of all the actions with which we have been engaged."

Indeed, discussions of spirituality are taking place everywhere. People are yearning for deeper meaning to sustain their lives in a highly competitive, violent world. The spirituality we seek must not only sustain us in this situation. The spirituality we seek must also be a call to move forward to act for justice in solidarity with the poor and the oppressed.

I glimpsed such a spirituality at a meeting sponsored by the Women's Peace Institute in Seoul, Korea. I was taken to the meeting by Lee Oo Chung, a human rights activist who lost her professorship because of the stand she took during the struggles of the 1970s. This meeting was a dialogue between women representing church women's organizations and women involved in the Urban Industrial Mission. The women involved in the Urban Industrial Mission are in their thirties, graduates of universities and seminaries. They live in the tiny, densely populated apartment areas where the workers live. Although at times they are faint from overwork and undernourishment, these women are sustained by their sense that the workers are people of God who can bring structural change to the society. They are fired by their conviction that these people of God have the right to participate in decision-making about production and to enjoy the fruits of their labor.

As these women involved with the Urban Industrial Mission talked, they explained how difficult it is to be whole-heartedly involved in the labor movement as well as organize a women's movement within the labor movement and not split the two. They are convinced that women workers need to organize. Women constitute about 40 percent of the labor force in Korea, and are paid an average of 48 percent of what their male counterparts are paid. They work an average of ten hours a day in the factory and another five hours a day at home. Despite their hard work, they cannot afford adequate housing: the space they can afford is almost unbearably small for their families.

The women of the Urban Industrial Mission are attempting to alleviate the hardships in the lives of these women workers. With this as their goal, they have started day-care centers through which they can get to know mothers and get them interested in their own education. The results are promising: strained family relationships change for the better when mothers are proud of the programs for their children and when husbands are proud of their wives' educational endeavors. There are about seventy day-care centers as well as sixteen study rooms that have been set up because children need space in which to do their homework, space outside the confines of the cramped apartments in which they live.

The women of the Urban Industrial Mission also testified to the interrelatedness of poor women workers and middle-class church women. Some of the poor women are dying from poverty; some of the middle-class women are dying from overabundance, from having too many things. In these mission women, who are themselves from the middle class but who have opted to work for the poor, I see the spirituality of solidarity. I see a new vision of incarnation as the movement of women and the movement of the peoples of Asia come together to work for the reign of God on earth.

Conclusion

We have seen the twentieth-century ecumenical movement begin to change from a movement begun by Western Christian white men into a movement more inclusive of diverse peoples and priorities. We have seen signs of a new phase of this move-ment in both the movement of women and the movement of peoples in Asia. But, even as we enter a new phase, challenges still confront the ecumenical movement. Too often the inclu-sivity is still token. Even though all God's people are disregard-ing the patriarchal guest list of participants in the messianic banquet, the theology of the ecumenical movement does not embody this reality. Moreover, we Christians in this new phase of the ecumenical movement are also challenged to be con-nected with secular renewal groups and with peoples of other living faiths. These people are also invited to the banquet pre-pared by God, whose household is open to all who will be in solidarity with those who struggle against the forces of death for the sake of life.

Searching for a Round Table
in Church and World[1]

Letty M. Russell

M OST of us are very familiar with round tables. We usually
find ourselves eating at them at home or in a family-style
restaurant or cafeteria. Round tables evoke images of unity in
communities of many kinds. Those of us who grew up reading
King Arthur and the Knights of the Round Table know that a
"Round Table" is that ever-elusive utopian vision of community

---

1. This article is based on a lecture on the unity of the church and
the unity of humankind presented at the conference called "Ecumenical
Moment '88: God's Call for Unity," held on 28 June 1988 in Stony Point,
New York. It is based on material from a forthcoming book by Letty M.
Russell tentatively titled *Church in the Round: Ecclesiology in Feminist Per-
spective.*

---

*Letty M. Russell, a Presbyterian, is Professor of Theology at Yale Divin-
ity School and is a member of the Commission on Faith and Order of
both the NCC and the WCC. She is the author of numerous books,
most recently of* Household of Freedom: Authority in Feminist Theology, *and the editor of a recent publication of the NCC's Commission
on Faith and Order entitled* The Church with AIDS: Renewal in
the Midst of Crisis.

worth every chivalrous man's exploits and every lovely maiden's broken heart. And those of us who follow the story of the ecumenical movement's efforts to live out church unity in Jesus Christ through faith, order, and service know that the Round-table Church is just about as elusive.

Yet the vision of the World Council of Churches' study entitled "The Unity of the Church and the Unity of Humankind" is different from King Arthur's vision in two respects. First, it is a vision already experienced through the table talk, table fellowship, and table solidarity of the ecumenical movement in many places around the world. Second, this vision includes not only knights but also faithful women and men of every tongue, race, and nationality. It is an image that compels us to anticipate now the coming Great Feast of God's eschato-logical household. At the outset I offer a word of caution about "following the gleam" of yesteryear with "banners unfurled o'er all the world," as we used to sing.[2] The image of the "knights in the days of old" still plagues the "old boys'" ecumenical movement as it moves ever so slowly—in the search for unity of the church and of humankind—to include women as well as men, poor as well as rich, and people of all colors.

During the Ecumenical Decade I would like to focus atten-tion on the image of the round table as God's eschatological banquet table where all are welcome, and to present some problems we might encounter and some clues we might discover in searching for a round table in the church and the world. Our search beyond these boundaries begins with a lot of table talk. Whether or not the tables are round, much of our time at church includes potluck dinners, coffee hours, and meetings where we gather to talk. At table we try to digest what we have heard and to plan what we will do. Gathering together day after day at communion tables, we discover "table solidarity," not

2. "To the Knights in the Days of Old," or "Follow the Gleam," lyrics copyright © 1920 by the National Board of the YWCA.

only with one another but with persons in every part of the world. And, finally, the hospitality we share overflows into celebration and anticipation at God's "Welcome Table."

Table Talk

All of us practice this habit of table talk for some very good reasons, including the desire to receive God's gift of physical and spiritual nourishment. One important reason for participating in table talk is that the Gospels present just such a pattern in the teachings and life of Jesus. Paul Minear has reminded us, for example, that for Luke "table fellowship as interpreted by table talk constituted the gospel."[3]

Searching for Unity and Renewal. My own table talk experience has been shaped by my pastoral ministry in the East Harlem Protestant Parish in New York City and by my involvement with the World Council of Churches and the National Council of Churches in various studies—"The Missionary Structure of the Congregation," "The Community of Women and Men in the Church," and "The Unity of the Church and the Renewal of Human Community." My present work as a delegate from the Presbyterian Church, U.S.A., to the Faith and Order Commissions of the National Council and the World Council is particularly concerned with how we are searching for unity and renewal at the ecumenical round table.

"The Unity of the Church and the Renewal of Human Community" is an unfortunate title for a study. If we are not careful, the title leads people into a false dualism which suggests that the church needs unity and the world needs renewal. This division of church and world is represented in the traditional

3. Minear, quoted by John Koenig in *New Testament Hospitality* (Philadelphia: Fortress Press, 1985), p. 86. Cf. Paul Minear, *To Heal and Reveal: The Prophetic Vocation according to Luke* (New York: Seabury Press, 1976), p. 83.

ecumenical movement by its too-easy assumption that theological issues of unity belong to Faith and Order and that sociological issues of renewal belong to programs of social justice and education.[4] Yet unity and renewal are both theological and sociological issues, and the church is as badly in need of renewal as the world is in need of unity.[5]

For some time the prevailing model in the theological search for unity has been the model of *unity through convergence.* This model struggles to deal with what are considered the most fundamental elements in church traditions about which some agreement is considered necessary. An example of this is the convergence document entitled *Baptism, Eucharist, and Ministry* that was accepted at the Faith and Order Plenary Commission in Lima in 1982. Along with agreement in apostolic faith and agreement on structures that make joint consultation and decision-making possible, this mutual recognition of baptism, Eucharist, and ministry constitutes what Lukas Vischer has described as the conditions that need to be fulfilled if unity is to become a reality.[6]

A more recent model of theological table talk in the search for unity complements "unity by convergence" by seeking *unity through contextual analysis.*[7] This model, which was the one used

4. Cf. the discussion of "The Community of Women and Men in the Church," in Melanie Ann May, *Bonds of Unity: Women, Theology and the Worldwide Church* (Atlanta, Ga.: Scholars Press, 1989), esp. pp. 59-88.

5. Cf. Letty M. Russell, "Unity and Renewal in Feminist Perspective," *Mid-Stream: An Ecumenical Journal* 27 (Jan. 1988).

6. *Baptism, Eucharist, and Ministry*, Faith and Order Paper No. 111 (Geneva: World Council of Churches, 1982). Cf. *Sharing in One Hope*, reports and documents from the meeting of the Faith and Order Commission held on 15-30 Aug. 1978 at the Ecumenical Christian Centre in Bangalore, India, Faith and Order Paper No. 92 (Geneva: World Council of Churches, n.d.), p. 30.

7. L. A. Hoedemaker, "Comments on the Relation between Situational Analysis and Ecclesiological Discussion," unpublished paper presented in Groningen, The Netherlands, Dec. 1985, p. 5.

by the study on the community of men and women in the church, is more open to the concerns and methods of feminist and liberation theologies. A continuing problem of the study on unity and renewal is the clarification of the validity of such a method in the theological search for unity, and the working out of ways in which this can complement rather than compete with the agenda of convergence in the search for unity of the church.

Roundtable Talk. New styles of table talk are badly needed if we are going to deal with the diversity of the world in which we live. Here I would like to suggest that focusing on the contextual analysis aspect of ecumenical table talk can lead us to some valuable clues in our search for a round table.

In Mark 7:24-30 we read that Jesus came to see his ministry differently when he was confronted by the Syro-Phoenician woman. The woman refused to accept the remark attributed to Jesus that as a Gentile she should not expect to be fed at the table. Determined to obtain his gift of healing for her daughter, the woman said, "Yes, Lord; yet even the dogs under the table eat the children's crumbs." Whatever we make of this difficult story, we can at least see that its intent in the early church was to expand the paradigm of exclusion and inclusion.[8] Today we need to do the same. We need to invite those who have had only the crumbs to sit at the table—not only to eat but also to talk and to teach us about the meaning of unity and renewal in their lives.

The model of contextual analysis is a very practical and accessible way of doing theology at the grass roots, but at the same time it is difficult because it requires a commitment to action for social change and a critical consciousness that is always seeking to make connections between theology and what

8. Sharon H. Ringe, "A Gentile Woman's Story," in *Feminist Interpretation of the Bible,* ed. Letty M. Russell (Philadelphia: Westminster Press, 1985), pp. 65-72.

is happening in people's lives. In the working group on unity and renewal in the National Council's Commission on Faith and Order, we have discovered that this model of theological reflection is key to our work. Using a model of engagement/ reflection, we have sought out groups engaged in human renewal to discover how understanding of the unity and mission of the church shifts in contexts in which people are struggling for their lives.[9]

The critical principle for discernment in our contextual study of ecclesiology is that discernment take place through the prism of communities of faith and struggle. We ask those communities what they have to say about the meaning of church life, and it is their insights and questions about the nature of the church that become the impetus for our continuing theological reflection. This is not a new principle for theology and ecclesiology; it is already present in the parable of the kingdom. Christ promises to be with the "least of these" at the break points of life. "For the church to be a sign of the kingdom it must discern its unity and mission at these points."[10]

This style of theologizing in a continuing spiral of engagement/reflection begins with commitment to the task of God's mission with those who are struggling for justice and full humanity. It continues with the sharing of experiences of commitment and struggle in a concrete context of engagement. Finally, the theological spiral leads to a critical analysis of the mission context that seeks to understand the social and historical factors that affect the community of struggle. Out of this commitment, this sharing of experiences, and this social

9. "Study of the Unity of the Church and the Renewal of Human Community, COFO/NCCC," unpublished summary of the working group process of 1985-1987, produced in Mar. 1988.

10. Robert J. Schreiter, "The Marks of the Church and the Renewal of Human Community," unpublished paper of the COFO/NCCC, Oct. 1987, p. 7.

analysis come questions for biblical and church tradition. These questions can help us gain new insight into the meaning of church unity from the perspective of the oppressed. Accordingly, this new understanding of tradition gives us clues for action, for celebration, and for further reflection in the continuing theological spiral.

Roundtable Talk Makes Connections. Because the method of contextual analysis often begins with case studies, it is likely to involve asking different questions about ecclesiology and to yield different problems. These different questions and issues are not at all easy to relate to traditional doctrines on ecclesiology. As Barbara Brown Zikmund put it in her paper entitled "Reflections on the Nature of Church Unity," "A contextual methodology (which we have followed) has more difficulty finding unity, but it remains open to the realities of particularity and diversity."[11]

Using the theological spiral as a contextual method can help us to make the crucial connections between experience, social analysis, tradition, and action so that all these different components are joined together in theological reflection within communities of faith and struggle. Instead of seeing the components as competing with each other, we recognize all the components as essential to the wholeness of theology. Such table talk in a theological spiral helps us to connect our own contexts with the search for unity of the church and of humankind. For this reason its practice yields us our first clue about a roundtable church. Roundtable talk that uses a contextual spiral of action/reflection makes connections between faith and life.

11. Zikmund, "Reflections on the Nature of Church Unity," unpublished paper of the COFO/NCCC, Oct. 1987, p. 1. See also Letty M. Russell, *Changing Contexts of our Faith* (Philadelphia: Fortress Press, 1985).

Table Solidarity

The connection between faith and life is very important because
people are quick to ask us not only about the unity we seek but
also about the unity in community that we practice in our lives.
In fact, table talk about the way God is at work in the world
to bring about peace, justice, and the mending of creation is
bound together with table solidarity—sitting where others sit
and standing where others stand in their struggles for life.

Searching for Unity and Renewal. The working group of the
unity and renewal study of the World Council of Churches has
been following a sort of theological spiral combining both a
consensus and a contextual theological model. It began its work
with a consultation on ecclesiology in order to shape the doctrinal issues of the study around the theme of what it calls "The
Church as Mystery and Prophetic Sign."[12] It has continued to
work contextually through the publication of a study guide for
local groups and through international consultations focusing
on how issues of sexism, injustice, and racism fracture the
ecclesial and social communities in which we live.

As one of many follow-ups to the study of the community
of women and men in the church, material on the issues of
sexism has been published in a volume entitled *Beyond Unity-
in-Tension.* We now welcome new publications as we work on
the international task of moving churches to stand in solidarity
with women during the Ecumenical Decade.[13] Publications on
the ecclesiological significance of the churches and their involvement in issues of justice are beginning to report on recent

12. *Church, Kingdom, World: The Church as Mystery and Prophetic Sign,*
Faith and Order Paper No. 130, ed. Gennadios Limouris (Geneva: World
Council of Churches, 1986).

13. *Beyond Unity-in-Tension; Unity, Renewal and the Community of Women
and Men,* Faith and Order Paper No. 138, ed. Tom Best (Geneva: World
Council of Churches, 1986). See also "Introducing the Ecumenical Decade
for Churches in Solidarity with Women," *Ecumenical Review* 40 (Jan. 1988).

meetings in Singapore in November 1986; in Pôrto Alegre, Brazil, in November 1987; and in New York in August 1988.[14]

What are all these consultations pointing to? Basically to the inseparability of unity and justice. As the Singapore Consultation declared, the church that neglects to confront oppression denies its own nature. There can be no quest for visible unity that denies the walls of division created by injustice within the church and the human community. The task is not made easier by the factions that such a declaration and such a stance create: new divisions open up in the church between those who stand in solidarity with the oppressed and those who preserve their privilege by withdrawing from church involvement in the world. Yet the task becomes a farce if it ignores these divisions and asks only about the divisions in earlier centuries of church history.

Reports from Latin America and many other places indicate that the struggles for justice and life not only cause new divisions and theological problems; they also provide us with new concrete models of ecumenism at work as communities join together in solidarity and hope. Thus the report from Pôrto Alegre says,

> This new kind of ecumenism, usually practiced around concrete issues (such as land reform, housing, neighborhood action, human rights), is also the opportunity for celebration. Thus the search for the unity of the churches has been challenged and enriched by this commitment to justice for the poor. . . . That new ecumenicity in the church of the poor makes room for new confidence, for sharing a common challenge and responsibility for a new situation and meaningful ways to deal with those differences of doctrine and practice which still divide us.[15]

14. "Unity and Renewal: The Ecclesiological Significance of the Churches; Involvement in Issues of Justice," *Mid-Stream: An Ecumenical Journal* 27 (Jan. 1988): 77-81.

15. Pôrto Alegre Report, unpublished Faith and Order report (Geneva: World Council of Churches, Feb. 1988), p. 9.

Roundtable Solidarity. When we look more closely at this roundtable solidarity among churches of faith and struggle, we discover that new models of church life are taking form both within and alongside of the church. These models are not necessarily the cause of disunity, for they help us to understand the way Christians are coming together in witness to the needs of their own communities.[16] These models often take the form of confessing churches in which people struggle to express their faith in the context of social and ecclesiastical domination.[17] The churches are concerned for people on the underside of social structures. They are committed to engagement at local levels in concrete-action projects that are also connected to wider movements for social change. Such models offer the possibility of partnership as persons who have never before been aware of the connections of faith and action begin to join with others to work for change.

Three such models that have been important in the search for unity and renewal are the feminist Christian communities, the Christian base communities, and the Minjung churches in Korea. In discussing these three models, I draw on my own experiences with such ecclesial communities as well as on the reports (of the unity and renewal study) to which I have already referred.[18]

Feminist Christian communities are part of the worldwide movement of women for full participation in the social, cultural, political, and economic institutions in the ecclesial and cultural

16. Letty M. Russell, "Partnership in Models of Renewed Community," *Ecumenical Review* 40 (Jan. 1988): 16-26.

17. Letty M. Russell, "Forms of a Confessing Church Today," *Journal of Presbyterian History* 61 (Spring 1983): 99-109.

18. See especially the report from the task force in Costa Rica by Mortimer Arias and the earlier report from the ad hoc group on racism, sexism, and classism by Letty M. Russell. These materials are unpublished but available from this address: Minutes of the Study on the Unity of the Church and the Renewal of Human Community, COFO/NCCC, 475 Riverside Drive, New York, NY 10115.

contexts in which they live. Many Christian women who are part of this ferment of freedom are forming women-churches, as Rosemary Radford Ruether calls them, and other alternative feminist communities that at once critique the patriarchal church and provide liturgical space where study and celebration can be inclusive and participatory.[19] These feminist communities concretize unity-in-tension: they feel forced to move outside the church in order to use forms of inclusive language and ritual that are resisted in most institutional church settings. Although they stand together in solidarity with women of all classes, races, and cultures, most of these feminist communities in the United States are made up of white, middle-class women who seek room to express their spirituality as women.

Christian base communities are not so different from feminist Christian communities: at least 80 percent of their members are women, and the grass-roots leadership is most often women as well. Julio de Santa Ana, whom Elsa Tamez interviewed for her book entitled *Against Machismo*, argues that the reason the majority of persons in the Christian base communities in Brazil are poor women is that these women find some freedom there that they do not find elsewhere in society.[20] These communities are an integral part of the movement for renewal within the Roman Catholic Church and for liberation throughout Latin America and in other parts of the world.

Although there are base communities in Latin America that are organized around the option for the poor but are not connected with the church, the Christian base communities have become the infrastructure of the church itself through their commitments: they seek to reflect on the gospel in light of their

19. See Ruether, *Women-Church: Theology and Practice of Feminist Liturgical Communities* (San Francisco: Harper & Row, 1985).

20. *Against Machismo,* ed. Elsa Tamez (Oak Park: Meyer/Stone Books, 1987), p. 18. See also *With Passion and Compassion: Third World Women Doing Theology,* ed. Virginia Fabella, M.M., and Mercy Amba Oduyoye (Maryknoll, N.Y.: Orbis Books, 1988).

commitment to create a just society, they gather for Bible study, and they share sacraments and concrete-action projects. Leonardo Boff underscores the connection between the Christian base communities and the church in his book entitled *Ecclesiogenesis: The Base Communities Reinvent the Church.* He writes, "For us, the basic church community is the church itself, the universal sacrament of salvation, as it continues the mission of Christ—Prophet, Priest, and Pastor. This is what makes it a community of faith, worship, and love. Its mission is explicitly expressed on all levels—the universal, the diocesan, and the local or basic."[21]

Minjung churches are beginning to emerge in many parts of Korea, especially in Seoul, as a response to the movement for democracy, peace, and unification. These churches build on the Minjung theologians' articulation of the uniqueness of Christian witness in Korean cultural and political circumstances. The churches have been formed by "second generation" Minjung theologians who want to do their theology in solidarity with the oppressed and suffering workers of Korea. Minjung churches include men and women; there are even feminist Minjung churches, such as the one I attended in the factory area of Seoul in January 1988.[22] In fact, they are like the feminist Christian communities in that they were initially constituted by educated, middle-class Koreans who chose to organize churches in solidarity with the workers and to devote their time and resources to the cause of justice. In certain ways, however, the Minjung churches are different from both the feminist Christian com-

21. Boff, quoting Jose Marins in *Ecclesiogenesis: The Base Communities Reinvent the Church* (Maryknoll, N.Y.: Orbis Books, 1986), p. 12.
22. These observations are based on visits to Minjung churches and conversations with Dr. Kim Yong-Bock, along with other Minjung theologians, during a Yale Divinity School travel seminar to Korea in January 1988. See *Minjung Theology: People as the Subjects of History,* ed. by the Commission on Theological Concerns of the Christian Conference of Asia (Maryknoll, N.Y.: Orbis Books, 1983).

munities and the Christian base communities. They are sponsored by various denominations as mission and outreach projects in which members work for social justice and lead worship. But because they are a small minority in a conservative church context, they exist more on the margins of church life than do the base communities, yet they are not altogether independent like the feminist communities.

Roundtable Solidarity Requires Justice. When we think of the great variety represented by these three contextual models, it becomes clear that churches whose form follows the function of God's mission with those at the margins of life need table talk and action that grows out of the needs of the people. These marginalized people contribute new insights into what it takes to work toward the unity of the church and the unity of humankind. From their perspective it seems clear that roundtable solidarity calls for a church that lives out the mark of justice. The church witnesses to the cross by standing shoulder to shoulder with those who are marginalized, by sharing their burdens and suffering, and by learning to live in community with one another.[23] The church's marks of oneness, holiness, catholicity, and apostolicity are to be shaped by the commitment to work for justice. Such a stance, articulated in many emerging church communities, gives us our second clue about a roundtable church. If roundtable talk makes connections, roundtable solidarity also requires the church to struggle for justice in the human community.

Table Partnership

Lastly, the implication of table talk and table solidarity is that the round table must also require movement toward table part-

23. See Jürgen Moltmann, *The Power of the Powerless* (San Francisco: Harper & Row, 1983), pp. 170ff. See also Moltmann, *The Church in the Power of the Spirit* (San Francisco: Harper & Row, 1977), chap. 6: "Marks of the Church," pp. 337-61.

nership. Coming together as partners around the table is a key ingredient in our search for a roundtable church.

Searching for Unity and Renewal. Those involved in the study on unity and renewal are still trying to work out how such partnerships can be formed, not only as a fabric for unity within churches but as a fabric for global participation in "peace, justice and the integrity of creation."

There are many reasons for the lack of partnership or koinonia, as Michael Kinnamon points out in his book entitled *Truth and Community: Diversity and Its Limits in the Ecumenical Movement.*[24] In the working group of the unity and renewal study being done by the National Council's Commission on Faith and Order, we are wrestling with this many-sided question of partnership in diversity as we study what the church can be taught by communities ministering with persons living with AIDS. We are preparing a series of case studies written by persons with AIDS and researching the literature on the ministry of the church in this area. Working with both denominational and ecumenical consortiums, we hope to build on an earlier case study by Jenny Boyd Bull concentrating on the Metropolitan Community Churches' ministry with persons living with AIDS. By doing so we hope to offer the church crucial theological reflection as well as to identify the key questions and issues being raised for church unity.[25]

Clearly, issues of sexuality, death and dying, health care, and the rights of gays and lesbians—to name but a few—are at stake here. We cannot talk about partnership at the table of the Lord and at every other table without beginning to face these issues and to form new partnerships with the gay and lesbian communities so marginalized by most church institutions.

24. Kinnamon, *Truth and Community: Diversity and Its Limits in the Ecumenical Movement* (Grand Rapids: Wm. B. Eerdmans, 1988).

25. Bull, "Aids, Homophobia and the Church," unpublished paper of the COFO/NCCC, Apr. 1986.

One of the key obstacles in finding our way to partnership and participation around the table is what has been called "the double sin of the church." Put simply, most of our churches cannot respond to the need for justice and liberation as a basis of partnership because they have reversed Paul's teaching that Christians need to be in but not of the world. According to Robin Scroggs, Paul reminded the Corinthians that they were to continue to participate in the life of their communities, but they were also to live as if the new creation were already at hand (1 Cor. 7:29-31).[26] Most churches today, however, are of the world but not in the world. The structures, class divisions, and prejudices that mark their lives reflect the culture of which they are a part rather than the new creation. Preoccupied with their own agenda, these churches refuse to be involved in social, economic, and political advocacy for justice among the nations. Only true repentance and willingness to be in but not of the world will lead churches to sit down at the table with those who suffer.

Roundtable Partnership. This change of heart begins at the "Welcome Table." In the tradition of the black church, this is the communion table and every other church gathering at table. At God's table those who have been denied access to the tables of the rich white masters are welcomed and offered a foretaste of the final moment of full partnership with God. In one of her early stories, "The Welcome Table," Alice Walker preaches this powerful message when she tells the tale of an old black woman who, upon being thrown out of the white church where she had tried to pray, met up with Jesus on a hot, dusty road. She walked and talked with Jesus—for how long, no one knows. But it was at least long enough for her to find her way home to God's table. Her body was found alongside the road the next day.[27]

26. Scroggs, *Paul for a New Day* (Philadelphia: Fortress Press, 1977), p. 52. See also Kinnamon, *Truth and Community,* p. 37.

27. Walker, "The Welcome Table," in *In Love and Trouble: Stories of Black Women* (New York: Harcourt Brace Jovanovich, 1967), pp. 81-87.

Roundtable Partnership Makes Everyone Welcome. In the romantic version of the "knights in the days of old" and their round table, we are seldom told about the slaughter of peasants and serfs—those sacrificed needlessly in the exploits of the knights. In a roundtable church, by contrast, the revision of partnership begins by welcoming those at the bottom and learning about their story and their vision of God's table. This contrast points to our last clue in the search for a roundtable church. *Make sure you have a welcome table.* Remember that the table is a foretaste of God's future. The table belongs to God, for whom all things are common. Having prepared for the table, we discern Christ's body not only in the broken bread but also in the broken people of the world. And if we welcome them to join us, we may receive the gift of a new church—a church in the round that makes outsiders welcome as they sing, "We're gonna sit at the welcome table one of these days!"

A poem by Chuck Lathrop, "In Search of a Roundtable," captures this vision very well. The words are an invitation to all of us to help with the preparation of God's eschatological banquet table:

> Roundtabling means
> being with,
> a part of,
> together, and one.
>
> It means
> room for the Spirit
> and gifts
> and disturbing profound peace for all . . .[28]

---

28. Lathrop, "In Search of a Roundtable," in *A Gentle Presence* (Washington: ADOC, 1977), pp. 5-8.

Toward a Common Confession of the Apostolic Faith Today

Mary Tanner

THE World Council of Churches is committed to working for the unity of the church. It has been suggested that three features will characterize a visibly united church: the common confession of the apostolic faith; the full mutual recognition of baptism, the Eucharist, and the ministry; and common ways of decision-making and teaching authoritatively.[1] Increasingly, it has been recognized that this threefold agenda must not be separated from the unity and renewal of the human community of the church. A united church in which ecclesial divisions were

---

1. See the report of Issue Group II, "Taking Steps Toward Unity," in *Gathered for Life: Official Report, VI Assembly, World Council of Churches*, ed. David Gill (Grand Rapids: Wm. B. Eerdmans, 1983), p. 45.

Mary Tanner is Theological Secretary for the Board for Mission and Unity of the General Synod of the Church of England. She is also Vice-Moderator of the WCC's Commission on Faith and Order, a member of the Anglican–Roman Catholic International Commission, and a member of the Eames Commission on Women and the Episcopate established by the Archbishop of Canterbury.

overcome but in which divisions based upon race, class, sex, or wealth remained would not be a church truly united. The church must be renewed into unity.

This has profound consequences for our understanding of each of the three features of visible unity. It is not simply that the community confessing its faith together must go out to heal the divisions of the world but that the words in which that community confesses its faith must themselves carry a vision of renewal and unity. The words of our faith must not prop up or reinforce divisions in human community. Likewise, the language and symbols of our liturgy must proclaim and image wholeness. Our agreements on ministry must testify to the unity of men and women created in God's image.

Our structures of decision-making, which are the bonds of our belonging, must include and embrace, not dominate or restrict; they must themselves point forward to the unity of the kingdom.

In the sixties and seventies the World Council of Churches undertook a series of studies on racism, the handicapped, and the community of women and men—studies which have helped to show the ways in which the classical agenda of faith and order is integrally bound up with the unity and renewal of human community. For example, the study entitled "The Community of Women and Men in the Church," which began by listening to stories of brokenness between the sexes, went on to draw from these stories various implications for every aspect of the church's life. This was a profoundly ecclesiological study. It showed how the church—in its confession of the faith, its language of liturgy, its exercise of ministry, and its structures of decision-making—sadly perpetuates the very divisions between men and women that the gospel proclaims are overcome in Christ. The message of this study was that a dramatic reformation was needed in the language of confession, in the liturgy, in ministry, and in church structures if the church was to be seen to proclaim wholeness and unity in its words and in its life.

Out of the study came a group report delivered at the now-famous meeting of the Commission on Faith and Order held in Lima, Peru, in January 1982. This report elaborated the challenges to the way in which the church confesses its faith. The second and third points of the report are especially welcome:

2. The trinitarian language of the Creed needs particularly careful investigation. How far are the terms Father Son and Holy Ghost/Spirit, which safeguard the distinctiveness of persons, still adequate today to describe the Trinity? How far should the contention of many women that this language excludes them from the community of the Body of Christ be taken . . . and lead us towards discussing new terms for confessing our belief in the Holy Trinity?

3. The confession that Jesus became man (anthropos) needs to be investigated to explicate the relation between the Jewish man Jesus and the risen, ascended, glorified Christ. Is maleness central to our perception of Christ? Many women are suggesting that the implication that maleness has been taken into the Godhead profoundly affected their understanding of their redemption. If the incarnation is thought of, as one speaker in Lima expressed it, as "enmalement" and not "enfleshment," then the implications of a male saviour are impossible for women to bear. An investigation also needs to be made [into] the way this affects our understanding of the representation of Jesus Christ by the celebrant of the eucharist.[2]

These paragraphs contain some of the major challenges from a feminist perspective to the church's confession of faith.

---

2. *Towards Visible Unity: Commission on Faith and Order, Lima, 1982*, Vol. II: *Study Papers and Reports*, Faith and Order Paper No. 113, ed. Michael Kinnamon (Geneva: World Council of Churches, 1982), pp. 48-49.

In response to the presentation of the study on the community of women and men in the church, Professor Raymond Brown acknowledged that "classical theologians may insist correctly that 'Father' and 'Son' are not sexist terms, but they must come to grips with the fact that, because of human experience, they are being seen by some as exclusively male." In listing a number of issues to be addressed in the future, he underlined the need to grapple with the question of "what is stated by God in the maleness of his Son."[3]

Since it is now almost ten years after the Lima conference, and since we are beginning another decade marked as a decade of churches in solidarity with women, it is appropriate to consider whether these sharp challenges of the study of the community of men and women in the church have gotten a response. Has a significant subsequent study, "Towards a Common Confession of the Apostolic Faith Today," been "infused" by the vision of greater wholeness that was glimpsed by the community study? Will it help women and men to be united together in a common confession of the faith, a confession that makes plain the equality, mutuality, and complementarity of those created and redeemed in God's image?

"Towards a Common Confession of the Apostolic Faith Today" is imaginative and creative. It aims to help the churches recognize the faith of the Church in their own lives and in the lives of those from whom they are separated. Moreover, it hopes that the churches, having recognized this faith, will confess it together. Divided Christians have to develop confidence in the fact that they do indeed believe the same things about the faith once delivered to the saints, the faith grounded in the Scriptures and to which the creeds bear witness.

The study of apostolic faith does not attempt to write a new

---

3. *Confessing One Faith: Towards an Ecumenical Explication of the Apostolic Faith as Expressed in the Nicene-Constantinopolitan Creed*, Study Document, Faith and Order Paper No. 140 (Geneva: World Council of Churches, 1987).

creed; the study is at once more difficult and more imaginative than that. With the Nicene-Constantinopolitan Creed as the focus, we are invited to go back, through the words of that creed, to the unique, normative witness of Holy Scripture. From this point we are invited to recapture together the faith of the church. But we are not invited to remain in the past. We are also sent forward to the present and asked to consider how we can confess the same "faith of the church" today in the face of the many perplexing contemporary challenges to the gospel.

The study is a demanding and lengthy one. It has three parts: the first focuses on explicating the Nicene-Constantinopolitan Creed in relation to Scripture and to contemporary challenges; the second works to stimulate the churches to recognize their fidelity to the faith in their own lives and in the lives of others and thus to renew their lives where they are unfaithful; and the third is intended to lead the churches to a confident common confession of the faith summarized in the creed. Explication, recognition, and confession form three distinct stages of the process of the study.

The first stage of explication of the Nicene-Constantinopolitan Creed has produced the study text entitled *Confessing One Faith*,[4] which contains major sections on the three articles of the creed. Has *Confessing One Faith* responded to the challenges of the study of community? Is it an instrument that will help to overcome the divisions between women and men in the church? Does it show that it has heard the specific challenges of many Christian women? In introducing the first article of the creed, which is a profession of belief in God the Father Almighty that uses the language of Father and Son, this text recognizes the fact that many women today experience such language as oppressive and hardly usable. Accordingly, the text asks, "Is it possible to understand and confess the fatherhood of God in non-patriarchal and non-authoritarian ways? Is there a way to

4. Ibid.

speak about God's fatherhood in a way which includes feminine attributes?" (para. 37). The concerns of Christian feminists are thereby acknowledged. But some will surely say that the very phrasing of the second question predetermines the answer because it points in the direction of ascribing feminine attributes to an essentially male and masculine God. Such a move means that what is male and masculine will continue to dominate and to determine all that is confessed about God.

In the paragraphs that explore the biblical background of the creed (paras. 42-44), important points are made concerning both what God's fatherhood positively implies and what it does not imply. God's fatherhood does *not* imply sexuality, nor does it imply that only those attributes which society has come to designate as masculine belong to God. Rather, God's fatherhood is seen as pointing to an essentially personal relationship between God and those who believe in God. It points to a parental relationship that includes, embraces, and transcends all that we have come to describe as motherly and fatherly functions. The text takes pains to point to the wealth of imagery in Hebrew scriptures in which God is pictured as a mother giving birth, suckling and nurturing her children. It also explores Jesus' use of "Father," underlining the way in which God is "uniquely his Father" when Jesus is in Gethsemane and on the cross. And the text indicates that God is "our Father" only because God is first the Father of Jesus. It is by adoption that we share in this unique father-son relationship.

In subsequent paragraphs of explication (paras. 48-55), a number of important points are added. With reference to "the image of fatherhood," we are told that the fatherhood of God must be understood in connection with the unique Son and the unique Holy Spirit. Although little is said about it, reference is made to the use of the verb "begetting" to describe the relationship between Father and Son. God's fatherhood is again seen to include maternal characteristics, so that parenting, not fathering, is primary. Moreover, we are told that to confess God as Father "is to acknowledge a wholeness in God," although this is a somewhat enigmatic and unexplained assertion. A final assertion is this:

> In Jesus's language about God "Father" is not only an image; it is primarily the name of the God to whom he relates. . . . In its function as a name . . . the word "Father" cannot be replaced. . . . It would no longer be the God of Jesus to whom we relate, if we were to exclude the name Jesus himself used. (para. 51)

An additional comment alludes to the fact that there is disagreement today about whether God may be addressed as "Our Mother," and that in such a discussion the distinction between image and name is important.

While the paragraphs devoted to the fatherhood of God evidence a certain openness to the issues raised by Christian feminists, they are nonetheless weak—for several reasons.

First, the text completely fails to communicate the fact that many women (and men) today feel alienated by the language of Father and Son. There is no acknowledgment of why this is so, of why some, who are neither stupid nor wicked, find it totally unusable. There is no acknowledgment of the oppressive patriarchalism experienced in today's world, a patriarchalism that seems to be entrenched and given respectability by the male, masculine language of the Christian tradition. This problem demands serious acknowledgment. Only as this is understood and openly addressed will a convincing attempt be made to redress the imbalance. At the very least such an acknowledgment might make the compilers of *Confessing One Faith* more aware of the excessive male and masculine language that pervades the whole text.

Second, although *Confessing One Faith* explicates the fatherhood of God in the creed in relation to some marvelously healing and complementary biblical language, it does not acknowledge the fourth-century context from which the creed emerged. It would have been helpful if *Confessing One Faith* had emphasized the point that in the debate with the Arians the main concern was not God the Father as such but God "the Father of Jesus Christ." Or the study could have set the text of the creed in its historical context with *The Homilies on the Song of Songs of Gregory of Nyssa* or the prayers of Clement of Alexandria or the writings of Augustine, not to mention the rich tradition of fourteenth-century medieval mystics; this would have provided corrective and complementary resources. These ancient resources help us to interpret the term "Father" in a broader way. Moreover, they give women today confidence to explore complementary images while not giving up on the use of the term "Father." If the study had made reference to the wider and richer ancient tradition which is the context for affirming the fatherhood of God, then the commentary might have been less negative about the use of "God our Mother," which is not a replacement for the language of the creed but is nonetheless an appropriate address in prayer. "God our Mother" is not a twentieth-century innovation; it is part of the tradition of our Christian past.

Third, the text does clearly say that the language of fatherhood applied to God is not meant to imply biological sexuality or maleness. But simply to assert this position is too facile; the matter is more complex. Society has, after all, gender-coded so much of our lives. Gender is associated with rigid categorizations and qualities in so many areas—human behavioral patterns, attitudes, jobs, even color preferences. We may deny the biological maleness of God and yet infer maleness by the language we choose to refer to God. A range of almost exclusively male gender-coded words continues to be applied to God, thus perpetuating the perspective that "male" and "masculine" rather than "female" and "feminine" are more appropriate to describe the three persons of the Holy Trinity as well as their inner life and relations. This needs to be clearly indicated if the language of Father, Son, and Holy Spirit is to be accepted by many women.

A fourth difficulty is the distinction drawn between

"Father" used as a name and "Father" used as an image. How does this relate to the Hebrew tradition that was firmly opposed to naming God at all? When Moses pleaded to know God's name, God's response was "I am that I am" or "I will be what I will be" or "I will cause to be what I will cause to be." God cannot be encapsulated in a single name bandied about by the people. The verbal form points to the reality that God is revealed in ever-new ways through interaction with God's people. *Confessing One Faith* needs to take account of this if it is to sustain its rigid distinction between name and image. Closely related to this is the underlying question about all language for God. To what extent is all language for God analogical or symbolic? We can never comprehend God fully, so all language, all symbols and imagery are necessarily fragmentary and approximate ways of referring to God. Regrettably, the study does not address these matters.

In short, the treatment of the first article of the creed in *Confessing One Faith* has gone some way to respond to the challenges of the study of the community of women and men in the church. But it needs to be strengthened, particularly by a clear acknowledgment of the alienating effect that male symbols and images have on many as well as by specific reference to various fourth-century and fourteenth-century traditions.

Unfortunately, in the paragraphs that the study devotes to the second article of the Nicene-Constantinopolitan Creed, the challenges of Christian feminism are hardly heard at all. *Confessing One Faith* does not comment on the phrase "eternally begotten of the Father" as a description of the second person of the Trinity. This phrase does not imply biological fatherhood but has to do with the matter of origin. That is, the life of the second person of the Trinity originates in the Father. The term "begotten" enables us both to affirm this origin and to underline the personal relationship between the first and second persons of the Trinity.

One paragraph on the second article (para. 112) underlines

the creed's affirmation that the Son of God became a human
being, *anthropos;* it goes on to explore what this humanity en-
tailed as witnessed in the New Testament records about Jesus.
What *Confessing One Faith* does *not* draw out is the significance
of the use of *anthropos*. This word was used to explain the
meaning of "became flesh" in John's Gospel. It was a way of
emphasizing the wholeness and thus the inclusiveness of Jesus'
humanity. It was strictly necessary for the sake of humanity's
salvation that Jesus be the same sort of being as those whom
he came to save. What is significant about Jesus becoming flesh
is not the specificity of male humanity but the common humanity through which comes the salvation of all.

Confessing One Faith fails to grapple with what God is saying
to us in the maleness of Jesus. In one paragraph (para. 113) that
explores the particularities of Jesus' life, the fact that Jesus was
a Mediterranean Jew is discussed, but we look in vain for a
healing statement on the specificity of maleness. This is a serious
omission. During internal debates within the Anglican Communion as well as during bilateral dialogues between Anglicans
and their Roman Catholic and Orthodox partners, this question
of the significance of the specificity of Jesus' maleness is a
recurring theme in the debate on the ordination of women. In
a recent report from the House of Bishops of the Church of
England, we read the following assertions, which reflect the
thinking of some bishops:

> Maleness assumed by God in the incarnation corresponds to
> something in the nature of God as he relates to us in a way that
> femaleness does not. Maleness reflects the fact that the initiative
> is always with God in a way that femaleness does not. The way
> God chose to be human is consonant with the basic nature of
> humanity as created by God. It therefore follows that only men
> can represent God in Christ as priests.[5]

5. *The Ordination of Women to the Priesthood: Report of the House of Bishops*
(Church House, Westminster, Eng.: CIO Publishing, 1988).

There could hardly be a clearer answer to the question of the significance of Jesus' maleness. From this perspective, the maleness of Jesus at once corresponds to something belonging to the nature of God and demonstrates maleness as more God-like than femaleness. It is precisely this kind of interpretation that makes women look for some clear statement on the significance of Jesus' maleness. What does the specificity of Jesus' maleness say to us? Does it indeed point to a truth about the nature of God, or is it simply a characteristic like the limited scope of his knowledge, like his confinement to first-century Palestine, and like the various other specificities of his life? Is not the tendency to exalt some of the concrete details of Jesus' life over others to miss the point of the Incarnation? Is it not to misapprehend the nature of divine revelation and, in the most proper sense, to espouse heresy?

When *Confessing One Faith* comes to the third article of the creed on the Holy Spirit, it includes nothing more than a short footnote commentary in response to feminist questions. In vain we search for some longer treatment of the Spirit that would balance what has become an increasingly male-dominated text. One paragraph acknowledges and then dismisses the questions:

> Because God's Spirit (Ru'ah) is feminine in Hebrew and related languages, some contend that the Holy Spirit must be considered somehow as a "feminine principle" in God, and be referred to as "She." The churches, however, affirm the scriptural imagery with its symbolic analogy and the use of metaphorical language, while retaining the masculine or neuter gender as traditionally used. (para. 185)

This academic and clearly accurate comment cannot be countered, but once more the study does not recognize that the Holy Spirit, the comforting dove, has for many centuries provided a compensatory, corrective feminine image in the Trinity. Jürgen Moltmann drew attention to this at the International

Consultation on the Community of Women and Men in the Church Study held in Sheffield, England:

> There is an ancient but suppressed tradition of the maternal office of the Holy Spirit, the divine motherhood. The Christian communities which were subsequently driven out of the mainline men's church found it natural to speak of the Spirit as the Mother of Jesus. In Ethiopian pictures of the Trinity the Spirit is depicted as a mother. The nuclear family—Adam, Eve and Seth—was often used by the Greek church fathers too as an image of the Triune God on earth, which certainly presupposes that the Holy Spirit is female and an archetype of the mother. Nor was it mere chance that Count Zinzendorf rediscovered the maternal office— the motherhood—of the Holy Spirit when founding the Pennsylvania Community of brothers and sisters in 1741: 'There is the divine family upon earth, for the Father of our Lord Jesus Christ is our true Father, the Spirit of our Lord Jesus Christ is our true Mother, because the Son of the living God is our true brother.'[6]

If the study had dwelt at greater length on this feminine tradition relating to the Spirit, a tradition that has become increasingly important to women, it would have balanced a discussion that by this point was overloaded with male and masculine language, symbols, and images.

Apart from the treatment, not altogether satisfactory, of the first article of the creed, *Confessing One Faith* hardly seems to have wrestled with the questions raised by the study of the community of men and women in the church. Yet, even if the discussion of each article were to more successfully address the questions appropriate to it, the text as a whole might still have avoided addressing questions about the interrelationship of Father, Son, and Holy Spirit—the male and masculine Trinity.

6. Elizabeth Moltmann-Wendel and Jürgen Moltmann, "Becoming Human in New Community," in *The Community of Women and Men in the Church: The Sheffield Report*, ed. Constance F. Parvey (Geneva: World Council of Churches, 1983), p. 36.

Confessing One Faith talks in more than one place of the relation of the unique Father to the unique Son. It is true that Christianity is grounded in history, and that we may not surrender the language of Father and Son for a new and rootless language, but this question remains: What is it that the relation of the unique Father to the unique Son safeguards that a relation of a unique mother to a unique daughter might not also safeguard? When the question is put this way, are we not forced to conclude that what really matters and can never be surrendered is the quality of personal relationship, is the complete conformity of minds and wills when the Son accepts the Father's will and embraces the cross? At the moment when the Son suffers the fear of abandonment by the Father, the Father suffers the fear of abandonment by the Son. The suffering God is not just the suffering of God the Son but also the unfathomable pain of God the Father, who for all eternity is love, as Jürgen Moltmann has observed. It is in the suffering God that we see the love of God. This is not power in the world's sense, not domination of the one and subordination of the other, not patriarchy as we know it. In these events we glimpse the very nature of God's being. The words "Father" and "Son" tie us to the Christ event, the event that is forever the heart and center of the Christian gospel. Because the Christ event is at the heart of our Christian life, the words which tie us to that event are not negotiable. But these events also transform and invest our limited human words with new content. We are forced to conclude that it is in the very uniqueness of the relationship of Father and Son that divine significance lies, rather than in any human concepts of fatherhood or sonship, however exaggerated and wonderful they may be.

One Roman Catholic theologian suggested that what *Confessing One Faith* lacks throughout is a Trinitarian dimension. A Trinitarian dimension would certainly have enabled the study to devote more attention to the exploration of the relationships of the three persons. Without this, the temptation is simply to

replace male and masculine categories with female and feminine
ones, producing the same kind of wrongheadedness in reverse,
or to complement "Father" with feminine images and attributes
that lead in the direction of a "motherly father" who may be
comforting to some but incomplete and unsatisfactory to others.
Only in the context of a truly Trinitarian dimension can the
alienation and pain of Christian feminists be healed. In the love
that flows among the persons of the Trinity—in this giving and
receiving, receiving and giving of perfect mutuality and indwell-
ing of Trinitarian life—we get nearest to a vision of God, who
is beyond the limitations of the male and masculine language.

"Towards a Common Confession of the Apostolic Faith
Today" is an exciting study. It has immense potential as an
instrument for drawing together those divided by Christian
traditions as well as those torn apart by human divisions. But
at this stage of its development it lacks maturity in relation to
the particular issue raised by Christian feminists. *Confessing One
Faith* fails to acknowledge the fact that a growing number of
women feel excluded and oppressed by the excessively male
language of the tradition for God. These women see the confession of God as Father and Lord as Son as serving to shore
up a church whose liturgy, ministry, and structures perpetuate
the inequality of women and men, though both men and women
are baptized as equals in Christ. The explication of the Nicene-
Constantinopolitan Creed needs to acknowledge not only the
counter-tradition of the feminine face of God in Scripture but
also the counter-tradition in the writings of the saints and
mystics of the church. Recapturing this tradition and surrounding the non-negotiable language of Father and Son with it can
offer a healing and nourishing resource.

Other tasks also need to be undertaken. In the explication
of the second article of the creed, we need to hear what is *not*
to be read into the specificity of the maleness of Jesus. We need
to hear that maleness is not a more God-like quality than
femaleness. Most of all, we need to see the Trinitarian dimen-

sion adequately explored. We need to hear about the limitations of the male language in each of the three articles that explore the Holy Trinity. We need to hear about the limitations that the male language of the articles place on the exploration of God the Holy Trinity—the God who is larger than this language, the God who is neither male nor female, masculine nor feminine, but who embraces, completes, and transcends us all.

Afterword

Patricia McClurg

L ET all the flowers bloom! That might well be an appropriate subtitle for *Women and Church: The Challenge of Ecumenical Solidarity in an Age of Alienation*. The diversity represented in these pages and in these writers is a many-splendored thing that is marvelous to behold.

This very diversity in a sense is like a bell tolling, beckoning to us and announcing our coming into a new era of women in the church and in the world.

No, this new era is not a time of church walls tumbling down or even shaking. Things are not at all okay with women in the church or the world. They are broken and have not been fixed—women are "still in but out" (Eileen Lindner), women's gifts are still being ungifted (Rena Yocom), and there is continuing alienation for women and so many, many others.

Patricia McClurg is a pastor in the Presbyterian Church, U.S.A., currently serving in New Jersey as the Associate Executive for Mission in the Presbytery of Elizabeth. She was President of the National Council of Churches in the United States during 1988-1989, the first ordained woman to hold the office.

194

Nevertheless, as women we are moving on. There is so much more before us, and in the midst of our reality checks we are working on what is yet to be.

Part of this coming into a new era is, as Melanie May puts it, our "coming to consciousness about our own differences." In the past we have been strengthened by sharing our all-too-common experiences of pain in the world and in the church ecumenical and the church denominational, sharing our experiences as well as our mutual hopes and plans for an inclusive church and an inclusive world. This collection of women's writings continues that tradition of solidarity but goes beyond it. Here we invite and implore ourselves and others to "receive differences as the prerequisite for solidarity," to quote Melanie May again. And we know whereof we speak. We've been on the road for a while.

The challenges to the church, to the ecumenical movement, and to men and women are writ large in this book. But there is no party line here. Besides lending support to one another, we challenge ourselves as women, as disciples, and as leaders in the church. There is no doubt that if the authors of these various chapters, together with those of us who are their readers, were given an opportunity to engage in discussion, the issues and hopes capturing our attention would be wide-ranging and the perspectives multi-colored. Is there and/or should there be a style of leadership that is uniquely female? What is and/or should be our approach to power, authority, and structures in the church, and how do we deal with the current givens? What a roundtable discussion that would be! (And Letty Russell gives us a glimpse of just such a meeting.)

The challenges to the church, to the ecumenical movement, and to men and women in the church are writ large in this volume. The two challenges which are clearest and most important to me are (1) that our caring about the church and the ecumenical movement and about women and men in the church must be for the sake of the world, and (2) that our caring

about the church and the ecumenical movement and about
women and men in the church must be for the sake of the
gospel.

"For the sake of the world" is a profoundly important challenge. "From my perspective," says Joan Brown Campbell, "the
unity of the church is inseparably bound together with the
renewal of broken human community." As women we know
something about injustice and what it means to be held captive.
We know something about the misuse of authority and about
the incredible power that abides in the status quo. There is
wisdom to be found in the pain of that knowing, and there is
hardheaded hope to be shared with each and every one who is
in bondage. At our best we will remember the loneliness of how
it was and is, and we will stand and walk with those who carry
burdens on their shoulders.

"For the sake of the gospel" is a second profoundly important challenge. "I believe this bond [of solidarity among women
across denominational lines] develops because, for feminists,
the truth of the gospel itself seems threatened by any theology
or practice that legitimates men's domination over women,"
says Margaret O'Gara. What a scandal it would be if we were
to stop or even pause at this point in our journey toward truth
and toward home. Our journey is for the sake of the gospel, and
it is for the sake of the world.

As I was carrying around with me the manuscript for *Women
and Church* (hoping for scattered fragments of time in which I
might read and ponder those pages), an inquiry came from a
colleague—"What's all that?" I responded with a brief description of the book-in-formation and my task relative to it, men-
tioning that this volume would be one of the many gifts that
would be offered up during the Ecumenical Decade of Churches
in Solidarity with Women. The not unfriendly but puzzled response of my colleague at the mention of the Ecumenical Decade was, "But I thought we had already done that." (Clearly
here is another individual whose name can be added to the long

list of those who, as Annie Machisale-Musopole puts it, "leave women to our own struggle.")

I in turn responded—and respond again today—"We have only just begun." The writers, editors, and other enablers of *Women and Church* have helped send us on our way.